COMPELLING STORIES, COMPELLING CAUSES

Nonprofit Marketing Success

SUSAN O'HALLORAN

TABLE OF CONTENTS

INTRODUCTION

WHAT STORIES CAN DO FOR YOU
AND WHY YOU MUST USE THEM

Simply put, our society wouldn't function without non-profits. From fulfilling basic needs of food, shelter, and medical care to artistically expressing the triumph of the human spirit – and everything in between - the quality of our lives would be greatly diminished without the work of non-profits.

Of course, you know this. You know your non-profit is doing wonderful things in your community. And, yet, you also know that the public, the press, future leaders, and even donors are just not hearing about all the lives you touch and all that you accomplish.

How would you like to take the incredible achievements of your organization and the positive impact your activities have in your community, and tell a compelling story that will -

- *clear up misconceptions*
- *draw even more volunteers and attract the best people to hire*
- *generate partnerships with other agencies*
- *create a buzz in the media*
- *enlist champions for your organization in the legislature, and with donors and foundations to bring in even more resources?*

Learning to tell your story and helping others in your program to tell their own stories - whether it's through speaking with the press, fundraising, enlisting volunteers, or even getting co-workers motivated and enthused - will give you the ability to communicate clearly while showcasing the goals and accomplishments of your organization.

I want you to be able to listen for those stories that will help you get more support, understanding, and goodwill in your communities. Throughout this book, I will be explaining The 6 S Story Power System™. From this 6 S Story Power System™, I want you to walk away with several story ideas that you can use right away. Furthermore, I want to confirm your hunch that knowing how to better tell your story can make a positive difference.

Why shouldn't you get recognition for all you do? Why shouldn't you share your accomplishments with others? I'm not just talking about ego satisfaction here; I'm talking about survival. Will your organization be around to continue its good work? How well you are known and understood has a lot to do with tipping the odds in your favor.

I am a professional storyteller, but that's not where I learned the power of story. I learned it from my Grandpa. When I was growing up, we would all sit on the front porch at night. Neighbors and family members found a place on the front porch stoop or brought their own lawn chairs. We didn't all have TVs back in the 1950's. We were each other's entertainment.

As I sat there night after summer night, I noticed a curious thing. The neighbors would be hosing down their sidewalks or digging small moats around the edges of their lawns or standing there with grass clippers in hand just daring a blade of grass to grow and, if my Grandpa came out and sat down, slowly everyone would put down their gardening tools and drift over to our porch.

Why? Because they knew they could count on hearing a good story. My Grandpa would tell stories, for example, about what it was like to make your move - trying to kiss your girl while parked with her… in a horse and buggy. How do you keep that darn horse still?

Or he'd tell how Al Capone's men used to pay the neighbors off with illegal booze in return for not mentioning anything about the still in the warehouse down the block. Some people would get milk bottles delivered by the milkman to their doors, but my Grandpa and neighbors would find other kinds of bottles on their front stoops. It was like renting a DVD every night to hear my Grandpa's stories. The movies played in our heads, and we stayed. And stayed. And stayed.

Human beings are wired for stories. In fact, we are story-making machines. That means you are, too. You simply need a system to remember what you already know. The blueprint for telling a compelling and persuasive story lives inside of you. We're just going to resuscitate it – release it and make it come alive. Most of all, we're going to turn your innate storytelling abilities into a conscious skill that is available whenever you need it.

What can a story do? Many things. It can create connection and loyalty, stir the emotions, make the complicated simpler to understand. But one of the attributes of stories that I think is crucial to the non-profit world is that stories build credibility.

Whether you're aware of it or not, people filter every word they hear through a "believability index". Many marketing classes will tell you that people are tuned into just one station: WIFM – What's in it for me? And yes, that's true! Of course people want to know what they're going to get out of any program or product.

However, even before your audience is asking, "What's in it for me?" they are asking, "Can I trust the person who is bringing me this message?"

Much of our influence is in who we are, rather than in what we do. We're so excited to rattle off all that our programs accomplish. Before people are examining the list of what we can do, however, they're wondering, "Who are these people telling me this and why should I believe them?" People filter everything they hear, see, and read through a credibility filter.

That's where stories can be so powerful: because it's not effective to tell people who you are or even who you are not. In fact, that only causes more suspicion. If you tell people how great you and your programs are, mistrust and, sometimes, even a little bit of rebellion surfaces. Someone says, "I'm the best thing since sliced bread!" Our brains automatically say, "Oh, yeah?"

If someone says, "I am not a crook", we think what?

"Crook!"

If you want to be believed and heard, you can't tell people who you are or aren't - but you can show them. When you show your audience who you are through a story, they are free to draw their own conclusions. The bottom line is, people trust their conclusions more than yours. In fact, they feel pretty proud of themselves for figuring things out. Their conclusions are more likely to stick because they feel they came up with the idea... and people tend to trust themselves more than other people.

The power in storytelling lies in the fact that when people hear a story, they aren't passively handed a scenario of what to think. No! They participate in the conclusion and, therefore, the story feels as if it's theirs. Anything that is connected with us is more memorable.

People remember some of what they hear and see, but much more of what they experience. You can't bring everyone you'd like to your workplace. But you can show them your workplace through a story that will transport them there, right into your office or field operation. They will experience your organization.

Think of the times you're deeply involved in a book or movie and, suddenly, someone comes in the room and asks you a question. You're disoriented for a moment. "Huh? What?" you ask. It takes you a moment to get back into the room, because you were somewhere else. You had been transported.

That's the power of story — you can show people who you are so that they vicariously experience what you experience every day.

So often when we feel passionate about something, we give our conclusions, our opinions, our preferences, and our great insights. We tell our audience what to think. A story, on the other hand, demonstrates how we got to our conclusion. It describes our journey so that people can take the journey with us.

Let me give you an example. In the Adult Education world, where people come back to classes to get their GED (high school equivalency certificate), many in the general public have the misconception that young people don't finish high school because they are lazy or shortsighted. Some people believe that folks who go back to school for their GED want the easy way out.

When we asked Joyce Fritsch of the Adult Learning Center for Leadership in Illinois why young people drop out of high school, she told the story of a young man whose mother had a drug problem and multiple partners in her life who shared her addiction. When she was entertaining a boyfriend, her son was not allowed back into the house until 11 pm. This young man had nowhere to do homework, nowhere to eat, and no chance for a decent night's sleep for school the next day.

What is your conclusion after hearing this young man's circumstances?

Do you find yourself thinking, "Well, it wasn't his fault that he never finished high school! The kid had no place to do homework."? Joyce

9

went on to tell us that when this young man got a job and finally had his own reliable place to live and study, he went right back to school. I'm saying to myself, "This boy deserves a leg up!"

Take a misconception you know people have about your cause or organization and ask yourself: What do I want them to be thinking instead? What conclusion do I want them to make? And, then, share a story that would lead your audience to that conclusion.

For example, Joyce might have thought to herself, "I want my audience to know that people drop out of school for a variety of reasons, most of which aren't their fault. I want them to see that these adults and young adults deserve our help, and that they can accomplish much with just a little bit of support."

From that clear communication objective, Joyce would think backwards. She can ask herself, "What story could I tell that would SHOW it often isn't someone's fault when they drop out of school, so that I don't have to TELL that to my audience?"

Here's another one of Joyce's stories. Let's say she wants to show the persistence of Adult Education students - how hard they work and how many just never give up.

Joyce told us in an interview, "One student came to us with a second grade reading level. She worked very hard, and came up to a fifth grade level. Then she had a stroke. We're back to ground zero - she can't read. She came back, and she worked and worked. At this point, she wasn't getting a GED to get a job. She was doing it for herself and her children. Then she had another stroke. That set us back awhile. Thirteen years from the time she started, she got her GED. It was a miracle!"

That would be a good story, yes? And it shows persistence; Joyce never has to use the word.

If I had the chance to work on crafting a story with someone like Joyce, I would take her terrific first draft of the story and, then, I would coach Joyce to not even say a little bit of her conclusion. For instance, in the first telling of this story, Joyce says, "It was a miracle!"

If that's her conclusion, I don't want her to say it. I want the audience to come to that conclusion themselves. So I would work with her to extend the story to, perhaps, two contrasting scenes — the before and after pictures.

For example, I'd ask, "What did this woman look like in the doctor's office when she had her second and third strokes? Was she unable to walk? Did she have slurred speech? What was her condition?"

I'd ask these questions so that I could paint the first picture. Without telling the audience what to think, I would paint the picture of this woman's difficulties in speaking and walking leading the listeners to conclude for themselves - "Wow! She had a lot of obstacles to overcome! She couldn't even hold a pen. She couldn't even say her own name!"

Next, I'd ask about what was said to her. There might be some dialogue with the doctors, for example, telling her that she'd never walk on her own again. Then, I'd coach Joyce to cut to the second contrasting scene, the After picture of this woman walking up the stairs of the stage in the school auditorium, using her cane, her body at a slight slant, politely refusing anyone's help as she reaches out for that diploma.

Tell the story so that it shows a scene and, then, let the audience reach their own conclusion that, "It's a miracle!!" It is more powerful for the audience to form their own opinion. They are participants in the story. Now it is their story, too.

Ask yourself, "What do I want my audience to feel, to know, or to do after they hear my story? How can I lead them there through images that they put together in ways that are meaningful to them?"

Not only do you respect your audience by allowing them to draw their own conclusions, you're giving your program a chance to shine, to show people how really important your work is.

I know a lot of us have shyness around the whole idea of persuasion. We have that stereotype about the sleazy salesperson, and we don't like the feeling of people being too pushy with us. What I'd like you to consider is that we are actually persuading all the time. Every day, you are persuading other people to listen to you or to ignore you.

You don't need to be pushy. You don't need to manipulate. You do need to be skillful.

Most of all, you can't assume that your job is already done simply because your organization does good work. The #1 mistake I see people in worthy nonprofit organizations make is thinking that their purpose is so worthy that everyone will get on board. But the truth is people suffer from "Compassion Fatigue".

Out of all the thousands of concerns competing for your audience's attention, why should they pay attention to you? What are the hidden treasures in your organization that connect to what your audience already cares about? You need to understand what's important to them, so that you can get their attention and communicate in a way that they can hear you.

What we know from the sales world is that people buy for emotional reasons and then they intellectually justify their purchase later. The way to make people care is to help them to feel something.

What you are trying to do is attract a community. You want to have a mission that's so strong, told through such compelling stories, that they create advocates for your cause. My goal is for you to market with your various audiences, not to them.

To repeat: you will be most successful when you can market with your audience, not to them.

I am going to show you my 6 S Story Power System™. That's a little play on words. Say "6S" fast enough, and it should sound like "Success" - because that's what I wish for you.
The Elements of the 6 S Story Power System™ are:

1. Story Setup
2. Story Speak
3. Story Setting
4. Story Star
5. Story Structure
6. Story Sharing

I'm hoping the alliteration will help you remember all the elements of a great story. The 6 S's can become a kind of checklist in your mind to make sure you're giving your message the best chance of being heard.

Many of you are already doing a good job of getting your message out, but you aren't using the full power of storytelling. Storytelling is really one of the best marketing and communication tools you have. You'll inspire others and, one of the best bonuses, you'll keep yourself inspired as well. As you tell your stories and bring out feelings of interest and caring in your audience, you'll feel more emotionally connected to your organization as well. Given the challenges of running a nonprofit organization, keeping your own passion alive needs to be one of your main priorities. The art of storytelling will help you do just that.

WHERE DO I FIND STORIES?

Okay, you're convinced. Stories are important and can do wonderful things. "But I don't have any stories," you say. Ah, but you do if you know where to look. I'm going to give you a series of categories to get you started. Spotting a story is a skill. I promise you'll get better and better at it.

I want to share with you just a small sampling of the kinds of stories that you can tell. When you see all of the uses of story, I hope you'll decide it's worth the time to re-awaken your innate storytelling skills.

When you want to tell a story, look for:

- **"Creation Stories"** – think of companies that started in the founder's garage, or enormously successful products or services that arose out of challenging times or even tragedies. These Creation Stories can become the stuff of legends. Make sure to interview your founder (or, if you're the founder, have someone interview you). It is essential to capture humble beginnings, passion for the cause, and obstacles that had to be overcome.

- **Identity or "Who We Are" Stories** – find examples within your programs and your outreach that depict your values in action. In other words, what are your core principles and when are you living them?

- **Mission or "Why We're Here" Stories** – show your positive affect on individuals, community, coworkers, and the world. When have you changed someone's life for the better? When do you know you are fulfilling your mission?

- **"Who I Am" and "Why I'm Here" Stories** – share personal stories of why you're involved in this organization. Who inspired you to get involved? Why do you come to work? When have you felt a deep satisfaction that you've accomplished something?

- **"Challenging Stories"** – describe times when the people you work for or with overcame obstacles. We all love to cheer for the underdog. Show when life looked bleakest and then tell the moment things turned around.

- **"Fresh Start" or "How I Learned from My Mistakes" Stories** – build credibility by admitting that you've made mistakes, have learned from them, and are acting on the insights you gained. Telling your audience that you fell short builds connection. You won't lose trustworthiness as long as you can show how being humbled helped you improve your product, your service and yourself.

- **"Unusual Connections" Stories** – relate an unlikely bond. For example, two men raised a lion cub and released him to the wilds of the African savannah. When they went back to see him years later, the lion did more than just recognize the men - he came running over a hill and about knocked them down with his two-legged, big-pawed hug. Or, at an Elephant Sanctuary, an elephant befriended a small dog that belonged to one of the keepers. When the dog got sick, the elephant refused to leave the gateway where his friend was being kept. The animal handlers had to pick up the dog and carry it down to the fence where the heartbroken elephant stood. Of course, these Connection Stories can include more than animal pairings. They may link the old to the young, the rich to the poor, the able-bodied to the physically challenged, etc. These stories are some of the most popular on YouTube and other video channels. Where do people make unlikely connections in your organization?

- **Surprise or "Man Bites Dog" Stories** – grab the attention of people with anything that is unexpected and dramatic.

- **"Right Now" Stories** – recount anything that is happening now. If it's timely and everyone's talking about it, it's likely to make a compelling story.

- **Local or "On the Homefront" Stories** – tell about something that's happening in your backyard.

- **Celebrity or "And then Lady Gaga Said..." Stories**
  – connect your organization to celebrity breaking news or
  an anniversary. You can fight the idea all you want, but
  people love stories about the rich and famous.

- **"Big Impact" Stories** – identify with people by
  informing them of something that affects a large group or a
  powerful institution.

- **"Nth Degree" Stories** – draw attention by talking
  about the first, the last, the biggest, and the best.

- **Success/Testimonial Stories or "Before and After"
  Stories** - influence people's belief in what's possible by
  showing that their dreams have already been
  accomplished. Success Stories make people say, "Wow!
  I've been thinking too small. I can accomplish even more!"
  Tell the stories of people who are the breathing, walking,
  talking proof that your organization's mission is doable.
  Teach the people you work with to share the obstacles
  they've overcome in order to achieve victory.

- **Future "In a Galaxy Far Away" Stories** - tell stories
  that begin with "Imagine if..." or "Picture yourself...".
  Help people to imagine something that doesn't yet exist.

- **"Stage an Event" Stories** – get people talking; create a happening. For example, you could create an event that breaks a Guinness world record. Or, give graduating high school seniors the GED test to show how difficult it really is. These created stories (when you're honest about the setup) can gain publicity because you've created a timely or unusual angle.

There are many other story categories, and many of these categories overlap. Let them get you looking for and noticing the potential stories that surround you.

The number or types of stories doesn't really matter. What does count is that you train yourself to look for stories. When you're reading the newspaper ask yourself, "Why did a reporter consider this newsworthy?" When you find yourself grabbed by a story on the radio or internet, ask yourself, "What kind of story is this, and do we have similar ones?" When you hear several people repeat the same story, ask, "Why do people feel this is worth sharing?"

Because part of the way I make my living is to tell stories from my life, people often ask me, "Do you just have a more interesting life or do you just know how to make your life into more interesting stories?" The answer is definitely the latter. How could I have hours of stories to tell about a pretty normal existence (whatever that is)? Because I've trained myself to listen for the stories, to play with ideas, to try them out and, then, see what I have.

You can do the same. The organization that can turn its reason for being into vivid, connecting, and engaging stories will rise above people's busyness and compassion fatigue.

Okay, these categories are for you impatient types who want to jump right in to find and create your organization's stories. But, now, let's slow it down a bit and examine each element of a winning story.

PART ONE:
The First S:
Story Set Up

CHAPTER ONE
YOU, THE TELLER

You will know the basic elements to storytelling – the six S's - backwards and forwards by the time you're done with this book. And that's a good thing. When you use these story elements skillfully, you will immediately increase your ability to communicate clearly, concisely, and powerfully. There will be times when you'll be telling one of your stories, and you will literally watch people hang on your every word.

"Well, give it to me!" you say. "Show me how!"

And I will. I promise.

But I want you to be patient. We'll get into the actual stories soon enough. The first S in our *6 S Story Power System*™ is so crucial that without it, the other elements of Story Power can't possibly work! I guarantee you that you won't be effective, no matter how great the story, without this crucial element.

And that element is your "Story Setup". If you are not clear and strategic about the Setup for your story, you may completely miss the mark and your communication will fail.

Here's what I want you to think of in terms of the Setup for your story:

You tell a story

To a specific **audience**

For a specific **reason**

In a specific **format**

Always within the **context**

Of your organization's **on-going story**

Sometimes, people think of stories as if they existed in a vacuum. But the Story Setup has as much to do with the kind of story you will tell as the people or events you want to reveal.

The Setup for your story has to do with the audience you are trying to reach and what you are trying to accomplish. In other words, you first consider your communication objective. You must also consider the spoken and unspoken agreements about the format and length of your story. In addition, take into account whether you're delivering your story in print, online, or orally as that will determine the type of narrative you tell as well.

And, finally, be aware that the story you want to tell always exists in the larger context of your ongoing story – the perception of and experience with your organization that your audience already has.

So let's look at the pieces of the Story Setup again:

> **You** tell a story
>
> To a specific **audience**
>
> For a specific **reason**
>
> In a specific **format**
>
> Always within the **context**
>
> Of your organization's **on-going story**

Begin with the first part of that sentence: "**You** tell a story."
Let's start with *you, the teller.* Your inner landscape is the first and
most important Setup for your story.

A lot of times when we think of communicating, we worry about
what we are going to say and how we're going to say it. But the
most important part of storytelling is *not* about what you say or
where you put your hands or what you do with your voice. There
is something more important to think about.

Your message and your presentation isn't just what others hear
or see on the outside. It's also about what's happening inside of
you - your frame of mind, how much you believe in your
organization and how comfortable you are with stating its case.

We communicate energetically with each other more than we
realize. If your audience picks up that somehow you don't stand
behind what you are saying, it doesn't matter how wonderful your
story is. You will first and foremost communicate doubt. You
need a strong belief in your story. You need to believe that it
deserves to be told and that it's okay to tell it and sell it. Many of

us hate that word "sell". The picture of a pushy, repugnant salesperson comes quickly to mind.

Instead, I invite you to replace that sleazy marketer image with your true experience of buying certain products or services. Are you glad that someone told you about certain items that you now love so much that you can't imagine your life without them?

Have you ever heard people talk about the coffee they love or why they only drive a certain kind of car or why you should switch to their kind of computer? These popular items make life easier, more fulfilling, and just more fun. If you like a product or service, generally you're glad that someone helped you discover it.

That's the kind of confidence you'll want to feel about your organization and its programs. People are going to be glad to hear from you and about you.

When you skillfully use stories, your audience is going to happily receive this word-of-mouth marketing from you. Trust me. They aren't going to feel as though you are twisting their arm because, through stories, you're never going to *tell* them what to think or do.

When you internalize that, when you've given yourself permission to tell your story, then I know that your voice, your gestures, your timing... all of that will follow quite naturally. You can always learn more about presentation skills from a seminar or one of our Story Power coaches. Wording and presentation will be the icing on the cake. But the cake, the most important ingredient, is your belief in your organization and your programs.

CHAPTER TWO
YOUR AUDIENCE

Now, on to the next part of the Story Setup sentence:

"You tell a story to a specific *audience*."

Audience! It's amazing how frequently they are forgotten because we're so focused on what we're going to *say* about our organizations.

Organizations often think of their communication with the wider world and start with their mission statement. Board or staff members go away for a weekend retreat to speak from their hearts about the passionate vision they hold for their cause. They are good people; they want to be inclusive, so they strive for consensus. Everyone's ideas end up in a sprawling paragraph or two. The whole process becomes unfocused and watered down.

Instead, I'm asking you to start by getting a clear picture of your audience. What do they already think about? What do they already believe and wish for? Speak to that – not to what you have, but what *they* want. Let your communications acknowledge where your audience is right now – their concerns, their dreams, the obstacles they face – and then find stories that lead them to feel, think, and take action in the ways you desire.

It all starts with knowing your audience segments. Are you speaking to a particular generation or ethnic group or profession? For example, a non-profit that runs a Divorce University is going to tell very different stories to attorneys to get them involved with their organization than they will to a newly divorced mother of three. You must know each of your audience segment's concerns in order to lead them to see that what you offer is what they're looking for.

I was just in a grocery store late the other night. I asked a young man who was stocking inventory a question, and I could see that he was really annoyed. He probably had some impossible deadline when all those cereal boxes had to be up on the shelves. He was totally caught up in what he was doing, what he *thought* was his job.

But the store exists for only one reason: for the customers to buy things. However, he saw my wanting to find something to buy as a distraction.

That's what many people do - get focused on the logistics of their programs. Getting them up on the shelves, so to speak. The brochure copy deadline is looming. Reports need to be sent. There are people to manage. We keep focusing on our To Do list, getting our products up on the shelf if you will, when there are people wandering the aisles – clients, donors, reporters, volunteers – looking for something and we're all but ignoring them.

What I am asking you to do in this Story Power program is to develop a marketing mindset. Now, again, I know some get squeamish at the word. We get afraid of being too pushy. Try this instead: think of a marketing mindset as a *service* mindset.

I want you to switch your brain around to give people what *they* want - what they want, not what *you have* – and realize that you provide them with a great service when you do.

For instance, an audience segment for many non-profits is local politicians. We're dependent on them for funding, yes? So I ask you to consider: what do politicians care about?

Getting elected! And how do they get elected or re-elected? By giving concrete examples that show they're listening to *their* audience, their constituents. They're walking down the aisles looking for "reduced crime rates" or "safer streets", and you're sending them to the aisles marked "Music Theory classes", "Little League", "Food Shelf", or "Divorce Clinic" – whatever is your non-profit's program and purpose.

Instead, tell them a story that shows a young man turning from the temptation of selling drugs because he got involved in your music or sports program. Then, have your statistics ready that show you're contributing to reduced crime rates and safer streets. If you don't speak in the language they're already using, it doesn't matter how beautiful your programs' packaging. It's not what they're looking for. They'll think your store doesn't have what they want.

We need to tell our stories in the ways our audiences can receive them. In other words, it's not a communication until somebody receives it, right? Too often we think about what *we* are going to *say* instead of "What are they going to hear?" I want you to switch to a *service* mindset and ask, "How can I help my audience find what they want and need? How are they going to recognize that I have something they want?"

Whether your audience is donors, volunteers, or agencies with whom you want to partner, you need to ask similar questions:

- What do they care about?
- What are some of the biggest problems they face? What is frustrating them?
- What keeps them up at night?
- What would be *their* –their- reasons for giving or volunteering or for getting involved with our organization?
- Are there misconceptions they have about our organization that we'll need to clear up first or along the way?

I hope you're starting to see from all of these questions that in order to be a good storyteller, you have to be a good story *listener*. Here's how:

- talk with them – ask them about their concerns and their current initiatives
- read their websites, press releases, and other publications – what are they saying about themselves and their objectives?
- speak with people who know or work with them
- find out about the other organizations they already give to, support, or work with
- support *their* events and projects
- examine the magazines that they read, and then asking those magazines for advertising kits that give the demographics and interests of their readers

Once you've done your story *listening*, then you can do story *matching*. Match the conversation that's already in your audiences' heads with a story about your organization.

I was working with an organization that provides education within a state prison system. The head teacher told me about a young man in prison. If she were speaking to people who are familiar with the juvenile justice system, the story she told me would work just fine:

"This young man got his GED in jail. His Mom and Dad had written him off. He hadn't been in school since he was in the 6th grade. Now he was clean; he was sober and had finished his GED and was applying for scholarships to college."

But for the audience this woman was going to address, this story could be the exact *wrong* story to share or, at least, the wrong place to start. She was going to address community people who didn't much like the facility existing in their area. They knew little about the prison system. Many believed criminals were getting off easy and their tax dollars were paying for a continual stream of handouts. She needed to ask herself the same questions you will ask:

- What conversation is already going on in their heads?
- Can I match that conversation, or do I need to create a bridge from their current beliefs to what my program does and whom we serve?
- What do I want them to think, feel, or do after my message is delivered and how do I lead them there?

People who work with prison populations know what a big deal it is for a young man to complete his education while incarcerated. Community people might need a wider context. I worked with the head teacher to slow the story down and spend more time connecting this young man's story with things her audience already cares about and *does* feel comfortable with. We worked together to create anecdotes that would make this young man more likeable by showing all the obstacles he had had to face:

dyslexia, the death of his older brother and so forth. We found examples of the parents, grief stricken from the loss of their oldest, frozen, unable to give their living son the attention he desperately needed and, finally, watching helplessly as their youngest son made wrong choice after wrong choice.

Remember, in this Story Setup phase, you have only one task: to truly pay attention to your audience. You could have the greatest prison program in the world but if in telling about it, you actually make your audience pull back – that doesn't fulfill your objective, does it?

People receive every message in terms of what they already know, believe, and care about. You can always bring an audience along - you just have to take care to bridge where they already are to where you want them to be. Never expect an audience to jump a large chasm. It just won't happen.

Eventually, the head teacher landed on telling her program's story from a totally different angle. She told the whole story from the parents' point of view. What is it like when your own kid, who has broken your heart a million times, finally turns his life around? Maybe your audience doesn't feel totally comfortable with the prison population yet – you're going to have to bring them along step by carefully planned step – but they do identify with a parent's grief over losing a child and their concern for their living son who, in so many ways, they feel they've also lost.

Remember, the same story can have many different angles and serve many different purposes, depending on the message you're wanting to deliver *and* the stories already in the minds of your audience.

In my Story Power Seminars, I teach something called the Elevator *Story*. Basically, a story is a problem and a solution. Imagine that you have a limited amount of time to tell someone about your organization. For example, you're at a conference and you get in the elevator of a tall building. There's already a person in the elevator who has the same conference badge as you. You smile at each other and this person asks you about your organization, How do you tell this person, in less than 30 seconds, who you are?

Here's the format I teach:

Hi! My name is _____ and I work with _____.

You know how... (problem)

Well, what we do is...(feature)

So that ...(benefit)

We're the only ones who...(unique service)

We're kind of like the...(metaphor)

For example, one day... (anecdote/story)

I know the idea of an elevator pitch can be overdone, but that's often because people rattle off their organization's mission statement in a robot-like fashion. In real life, this Elevator Story isn't so much a monologue as pieces of a conversation you want to have ready in your back pocket so that you can have a conversation with someone and, still, slip in examples of the kinds of results your organization delivers. But remember you'll need a different Elevator Story for each one of your audiences.

For example, here is an Elevator Story from an art museum in Ann Arbor:

"You know how people will be standing in a super contemporary museum staring at a wall of modern art, and they *want* to like it, but they don't always understand it? They wonder, "Why is that art?"

Well, what we do at the *Carnegie Library* is house a modern art collection in turn-of-the-century oak paneled rooms with fireplaces and comfy leather chairs. Our staff, who are people passionate about the art, might sit down across from you and share their enthusiasm and knowledge with you.

You get to relax, ask any question you like – just like you were sitting having a conversation in your own home. You leave our museum feeling tranquil, having had a great exchange and finally understanding just why some of those paintings and sculptures you saw *are* considered art.

We're the home-y museum with the feel of having friendly tour guides right in your living room ready to serve you. We open the curtains to a view onto a whole landscape of the art world that may have been hidden from you."

You could tell me quite clearly, I'm sure, the type of audience to whom this Elevator Story is directed. This description is to people who aren't quite sure about modern art, yes? This storyteller is making them feel comfortable. The museum, she tells them, is set up like a comfortable living room. You can get your questions answered by having a conversation with someone sitting close to you, not by having to stand up in front of a lecture hall filled with people who know art in a way you don't. But what if the teller was speaking to an art aficionado with his or her own collection of modern art? The Elevator Story would be quite different, wouldn't it?

Depending upon how different your audiences are, you may need to have several Elevator Stories as well as different communication campaigns for the same event or program. There is no "one size fits all" when it comes to communication.

SUSAN O'HALLORAN

CHAPTER THREE
YOUR COMMUNICATION OBJECTIVE

"You tell a story for a specific reason". When you think of your communication objective, you're really asking two questions:

1. What do we want our audience to think, feel or do?
2. And, then, thinking backwards from this objective: what key messages does our audience need to receive, understand and believe in order to perform these actions?

Think clearly: what's the outcome of your communication to be?

Do you want your audience to come to an event? And once there, what do you want them to do? Sign up for something? Get more information? Volunteer? Donate?

Do you want them to visit your website? And once there, what do you want them to do? Spend more time on your site? Download something? Donate? Read about you? Sign up for a free report?

Are you directly asking for contributions? How have you shown a need that connects with a person, a situation, or a cause that your audience cares about?

Are you trying to change an old perception of your organization or are you trying to be seen in a new and expanded way? Once you are clear on where your audience is now and where you'd like them to be, then, and only then, you'll search for the stories that will evoke the thought, feeling or action you desire. Sometimes, you don't know why you are attracted to a story and, therefore, what it can do for you. That's okay. Have a way to file it and find it later, when the purpose it can serve and why you want to tell it becomes clearer to you.

Sometimes, I think I know what a story is about and then, when I spend more time with it or see my colleague's reaction when I tell it, I realize, "Oh, no, that story works on a whole other level. It's not showing what I think it does!" or even, "This story is raising more questions than it answers. I'd confuse my audience, or open a can of worms."

Stories often reveal their meanings over time. Meaning can't be forced. Instead, spend time in reflection and in seeking feedback from others to see if your organization's stories are delivering the intended messages that will help you reach your communication objectives.

CHAPTER FOUR
THE FORMAT

The next part of the Setup for your story is to determine the appropriate format and length for your story. **"You tell a story... _in a specific format_."** Ask yourself, "How am I reaching my audience?"

Your communication objective drives the format or outlet for your message.

How you're reaching your audience makes a huge difference – whether it is done online, through a personal introduction at a social event, in a newspaper column, or at a business forum. When you consider the Setup for your story, it will tell you something about how long and what kind of story you can tell. There are many types of narratives.

A **simple comparison or metaphor** is a mini-story because it plants a picture in people's minds. It distills a complex thought into a comprehensible, easy-to-grasp image.

A **short proverb or fable** can be the most memorable and humorous part of your keynote talk or press conference. A proverb is a small snapshot of a piece of wisdom such as "an apple a day keeps the doctor away". A fable has a lesson within, often told with animals or characters with other worldly characteristics

– a leprechaun, a genie, or a magician, for example.

A **report** is story about what happened in the past – the kind of storytelling many of us do in meetings or for grant applications.

A **news report** is about something happening *right now*, and is a very different type of storytelling because there is a prescribed format that the media outlet already uses.

A **story pitch or hook** is a short teaser that should cause your audience to say, "Well, what happened? Tell me more." This can also mean telling your story via social media in 140 characters or less, and then driving your audience to your website for more information.

Next, an **anecdote** is a type of narrative that is an illustration or example. Even though it's a short story, it still has a beginning, middle, and end.

Finally, a **full story** is formed around a specific person with a problem that is solved or learned from by the end of the story. The main character wants something and she's not getting it – she has a problem. A full-out story has ups and downs of tension and twists of plot – what is called rising and falling action. The structure of a full out story, the seesawing of the rising and falling action, is what keeps the audience interested in the main character and action of the story. *Oh, now she's moving closer to her goal – now she's moving away from it! Now she's closer to her desire – now drat, she's not!*

At the end of a full-out story, there's a feeling of satisfaction because it all adds up to something. If not "happily ever after," some insight, at least, has been gained.

These are the main types of stories you'll be concerned with: metaphors, comparisons, proverbs, fables, reports, news stories, story teasers, anecdotes, and full-out stories. There are many other types of narratives: myths, legends, parodies, comedies, plays, but we've got plenty to work with here already.

Depending upon the audience and where you are delivering your story, you will pick the story format, the type of narrative you will tell.

If the newspaper reporter has a 300-word column, you aren't going to submit a 2000 word story. You won't tell a full-out story, but you will find one searing analogy or anecdote to make your point.

If you have two-minutes to deliver your message at a legislative hearing, you are not going to be heard once you go beyond that two-minute mark. It doesn't matter if what you share is the best full-out ten-minute story ever heard.

Twitter, Facebook, and other social media sites will let you know when you've gone over your allotted content. They simply won't let you publish any further words.

You can break through people's apathy by using stories in settings where people aren't expecting them. For example, you can use story teasers in your meetings. Instead of the usual one-dimensional agenda, "Today, we will cover a. the Fundraising Campaign Report and b. the Bike-a-Thon update." Write the agenda as questions, such as:

> A. Did our fundraising drive reach its objective? Is Joanne keeping her job? (You can add a little humor, right?)

B. What has been the most successful Bike-A-Thon in this city's history? Can we even come close to matching it (or, dare I say, surpassing it)?

Pitch the questions, again, to your audience by stating something they care about -something they are already wondering (the conversation already in their minds). Using story teasers can give forward momentum to your meeting, report, or video blog.

This technique is used all the time: You plan to go to bed, and then the evening news promotes their upcoming stories. They don't tell you the whole story. They only tell you enough to get you interested. And, darn! There you are, staying up 30 minutes later than you planned because you've got to hear the rest of the story.

Whether you're using story teasers or another form of storytelling, they often work because of what you *don't* say. Holding back some information, especially the conclusion, makes a story compelling.

Pay attention when you can't get out of the car because you're listening to a story on the radio. Enjoy the story, but start asking yourself, "Why can't I turn this off? What's keeping me tuned in, even though I'm late for my appointment? What *aren't* they telling me that I have to hear?"

I started this book with a kind of story pitch and a promise: "How many of you know your organization is doing great things, but people just aren't learning about it? And how many of you would like to learn to make your organization's mission come alive in a compelling story that would grab people's attention and make them *want* to get involved in your programs?"

In a story pitch, you're going for a nod of the head. You want your audience to respond, "Oh, yeah, that's for me. I want to know this."

Now, part of your audience's brain is tuned in - anticipating the conclusion. Your audience is awake. They're listening for the promised information that answers some need of theirs - some conversation already going on in their head. You can use these kinds of story teasers in your newsletters, and even when you start email or phone conversations.

There are always spoken and unspoken agreements in any communication. Parts of those unspoken agreements have to do with story length and format.

I will develop full-out stories for when I give a keynote address, or for when I'm doing full day seminars and I have time for them. However, I also have a three-minute version and even a 30 second version of that same story to weave into conversations or to share on a radio or TV show where the clock is always running.

By giving specific images, I still do what the full-out story accomplishes: I create word pictures in the minds of the audience members, and that's always more memorable than only giving abstract conclusions or statistics.

Keep in mind that, depending upon your Story Setup, you are going to need to develop a kind of versatility so that you can change the length of your stories.

"Oh no!" you say. "It's hard enough coming up with one story. Now, I have to come up with three versions of it?" Don't worry. Shrinking and expanding stories is a skill that will become second nature to you.

When you're choosing the right format for your story, ask yourself: How much time or space am I allowed? Is there an agreement that humor is all right? If so, what kind of humor? What's the agreement on how much emotion to express?

Your audience and the type of agreements (spoken and unspoken) that you have with them will determine the type, and therefore length, of story that you tell.

Lastly, remember, **"You tell a story... within the larger context of your organization's on-going story."** None of the Story Setup will work if the truth of your organization is out of sync with the stories you tell. Your organization is telling stories all the time. You have an on-going Story Setup, and that is how people see and experience your organization.

How do people become involved with your service? What is the timeline from when people are first introduced to you and, the string of rituals that follow? Are these positive experiences?

How does the way your phone is answered, the look of your building, your correspondence, your customer service, your website, your public meetings, and even your interactions with co-workers align with the stories you want to tell?

Is there a past image or story about your program that, even if untrue, needs to be dealt with? Every story you tell is placed against the backdrop of people's existing and ongoing experience with you.

No single story about how great your program is will have impact if someone has already had or is having negative experiences with your organization. It's important to understand what the stories you are going to create can and can't do.

You can tell the greatest anecdotes about your organization, however, you'll rarely get past the credibility gap you've created if your receptionist is rude to someone, if you told an applicant to send in Form A but they really needed to send in Form B, if your organization works with families, but your team never gets to spend an ounce of time with their own families and so on. If you make claims that turn out later to be untrue, your stories will lose their power. No story can trump your clients' experiences with your organization.

Your stories always rest in the reality and perception of your organization. Never expect a story or any other marketing tool to prop up something in your program that needs changing.

Yes, your image can be changed. In fact, you *can* build a lot of credibility from that story: How we've changed. Where we went wrong. What we're doing differently now.

That's a wonderfully universal story, but the change has to be real.

In the next chapters, we're going to look at the elements of a story that will make your stories immediately more interesting. However, don't overlook the hard thinking that has to be done to get the Setup for your story right. Create winning stories by first thinking through your story Setup. Remember, your story is being delivered…

To a specific audience

For a specific reason or communication objective

In a specific format of spoken and unspoken agreements on time and space and, therefore, the type of narrative you can tell

And always within the larger context of your clients' experience with your organization, your organization's on-going story

The most interesting story delivered with the wrong Setup is just not going to work. Although a retail store can offer you the greatest pair of size 9 shoes, you're not going to even look at what they have if what you're looking for is a wristwatch or a car battery or even a pair of size 7 shoes.

Pay attention to where and to whom your story is going to be delivered, *and* to what you want and can realistically accomplish. That's how your story will hit the mark. Clear communication takes thinking. Our society is not one that easily values or rewards reflection. The best storytellers are tuned into not only what they want to say but, first and foremost, to what their audiences will hear.

PART TWO
THE SECOND S:
STORY SPEAK

CHAPTER FIVE
SENSORY DESCRIPTION

The definition of a story can be summed up in one sentence: **You know it's a story when the audience you want to reach can picture a particular time and place where someone they care about faces greater and greater obstacles while trying to reach his or her goal.**

The first words of the story definition refer to what we've already covered: the Story Setup – the audience you want to reach.

The next words in our story definition "your audience…can PICTURE" refers to what I call Story Speak - the second S in our *6 S Story Power System*™.

To talk in Story Speak you must produce word pictures. Pictures. Pictures. Pictures. Your language has to create movies in the minds of your audience.

Story Speak is a very distinct type of language. It doesn't want to make you debate, it simply makes you *see*. Another phrase for Story Speak would be Story Snapshots. It creates descriptive pictures. It's sensory – what do you see, hear, smell, taste, or touch because of the story? Story Speak is not theoretical, opinionated, or abstract - it's concrete and specific. It puts you in a time and place where, in your imagination, you can watch something happen and react to it.

As we mature, we gain more knowledge and start to talk more and more abstractly. We spend much of our time in the language of statistics, theories, explanations, and opinions.

There's nothing wrong with that way of thinking and speaking, but Story Speak is different. It is a kind of language that opens up other worlds through sensory images. It gives people that "you are there" feeling. The phrase "… your audience can picture…" means that your stories give your audience scenes and places to imagine that are filled with relatable people and activities.

The reason that stories are so powerful is that our brains can't tell the difference between what is real and what is not. If you hear or watch a story about someone walking in the woods where a bear jumps out, and the story is told or shown well, your heart rate and respiration will change. Your body will prepare for flight, fight, or freeze - as if you were really in that dangerous situation.

You probably have known some people who love to go to the movies to be scared. They know the movie isn't "real", but their minds are tricked by the vivid images shown on the screen. For them, a scary movie is a safe adrenalin rush.

When I was a child, I loved reading stories about time travel. I wanted a time machine so badly! Then one day as an adult, I was journaling and writing about my parents. I was writing about what kind of clothing they wore – my Dad's flannel shirts and my Mom's plaid dress with the starchy lace on the collar and the edge of the sleeves.

I so remembered the *feel* of my parents as I sat on their laps that, even though they've been gone for many decades, I was so moved that I made myself cry! As I wrote and the memories welled up inside me, I realized, "Oh, my gosh! I *have* the time machine!" I had transported myself back to 1955 by writing a story of my parents with sensory description.

Over the years, I've made plenty of adult observations about my family: I miss my parents. I loved my parents. Our relationships were complicated and so on, but it was the sensory language that made me time warp back into the *feel* of being with them. The time machine is what reproduced my emotional reaction.

I do an exercise in my seminars where people imagine their childhood homes. What were the smells in your kitchen? What did your house smell like at dinnertime? What was the feel of your bedspread when you pulled it up around your nose on a cold winter night? Do you remember the sound of the back door slamming? What was the feel of your grandmother's soft cheek as she walked through the door and hugged you, her arms filled with holiday presents?

Sometimes, people will get tears in their eyes as they are remembering. It's as if you're back there, because your brain can be led to believe that you *are* there.

A good description will make your mind - and your body - think it's there. This means you can take your audience to work with you. You can put them in your rehearsal studio or homeless shelter, and cause them to experience your good work for themselves. You can put your audience in time and space machines, transporting them to see your cause in action.

Most people think visually. People retain about 20% of what they read, but 80% of what they see. If I show a class a slide of golden arches, most people will automatically think "McDonald's". Graphic images are memorable. But what is seen and felt in our imaginations and is just as powerful are the *word pictures* we create.

In the introduction to this book, I talked about how listening to my Grandpa at night on the front porch was like watching a DVD every night. He created movies. You can too. You can create movies for people by creating sensory word pictures.

Inventors have been talking for years about creating an experience in the movie theaters called "Sense-surround", where people experience much more than just seeing and hearing the movie - the seats move, the air fills with scent, the wind blows, the temperature rises and falls and so forth. But you've beaten them to it. You already have sense-surround when using descriptive, sensory Story Speak.

The way to make people care about what your organization does is to get them *to feel* something. However, people are less likely to feel if you tell them what to feel. They will feel when they have an experience, a reaction to pictures or to the movies in *their* heads.

Here's an exercise—grab some paper and, on it, I want you make two columns. In the first column, write all your theories, your opinions, your thoughts, your summaries, your preferences, your conclusions, your objectives, and your insights about your program or organization. Write out the issues your organization tackles and the things that you do.

In the second column, write Story Speak descriptions. How can you *show* that theory or opinion? What are things you see, hear, touch, smell, and taste? Write concrete images that *show* a preference, a conclusion, or an abstract idea.

For instance, in the first column, you might say, "The students at this University work hard. They are ambitious."

Then ask yourself: When and where do I see the students working hard? What do they look like? What are they doing?"

For the second column, you write images about how your students look like at midnight, hunched over books, studying at the library's extended hours after their after school jobs are done or studying on the train on the way to pick their children up from daycare.

I remember hearing Oprah Winfrey talk about bein depressed, but she never said the word. She never used that abstract summary, that adult way of talking. She said, instead, "You find yourself at 3 pm in the afternoon still in your pajamas wearing your fuzzy slippers, sitting on the couch watching TV under a pile of blankets while eating dry Cheerios out of the box."

Give a specific sensory image and what will follow is a cascade of memories and empathy. Oprah made the audience identify and participate in the image. She made them work a bit to conclude, "Oh, she's talking about being depressed."

Someone once told me that a 10 to 1 ratio is needed in storytelling. Ten really good sensory descriptors to earn the right to make even one summary statement, such as: "Our students work hard".

So, don't just say, "flowers." Talk about "geraniums" or "daffodils". Don't tell me a woman was "old." Describe how her body bent at a curve, her eyes trained on the ground.

I remember first becoming aware of true poverty when I was a teenager by reading James Agee's account of spending a night in the home of a tenant farmer in Georgia. He didn't simply write, "Oh my! These people are living in tough situations!"

He wrote of the house having the odor of old moist newspapers; shutters held together with string; crevices in the walls filled with rags, newsprint, and raw cotton. His words told of shivering from the cold wet air as he slipped into slimy sheets and, then, feeling sharp little piercings and crawlings along his body from the bed bugs. He described jumping up, lighting a match, and watching the bugs scatter only to see translucent, brittle insects that he took to be lice lining the seams of the mattress.

Okay! I was absolutely squirming reading his account of his overnight stay in the cabin. The writer, James Agee, didn't give his conclusion. He *caused me* to conclude: "Wow! These folks are living in tough situations!" *He described; I felt.*

One day in a seminar, I was doing a sensory exercise with my students. I had them close their eyes. I put different smells under their noses to see what memories various scents might evoke.

One object I passed around was baby powder. One woman, Joanne, took a whiff of the powder and started crying. Tears are always welcome in my class, and I asked her if she wanted to share what memory had come up for her. Joanne said that when she was a young woman, about 18 years old, she been arrested in Hawaii for carrying drugs. She was caught, convicted, and sentenced to a year in prison.

Joanne had a seven-month old baby at the time. She described for us what it was like to say goodbye to her son. She talked about burying her nose into her baby's neck as she held onto him, and catching a whiff of that baby powder smell. Her lasting memory of going off to jail was that sweet, sweet baby smell!

The memory had come back to her full force – as it can with scent. Everyone has had that experience of a powerful, full-blown, long-forgotten memory released from some hidden part of the brain at the faintest scent of something.

At the time of this class, Joanne was the director for a Chicago Legal Advocacy group for incarcerated mothers. She was going to pitch a story to the Chicago Tribune about North Carolina and other states unveiling controversial programs that would allow incarcerated mothers with children less than 9 years of age to keep their children with them. Joanne tied her story to a timely news item about a local political official going to jail (see Chapter Fifteen: News Stories). I encouraged her to use that very scene from her life when she talked to the reporter. Sure enough, that image of Joanne being torn away from her baby, smelling her baby for the last time as she was led off to prison, was the lead paragraph in the newspaper article.

> Seventeen years to the day before former Cicero town President Betty Loren-Maltese said goodbye to her 5-year-old daughter and reported to California federal prison, Joanne Archibald made a similar journey through the same gates. Archibald still remembers standing at the threshold of the Dublin Federal Correctional Institute and burying her face into the sweet-smelling neck of her 7-month-old son.

> "I just wanted to drink it all in," she said. "I knew it would be a long time before I had it again." While Loren-Maltese publicly anguished over what would happen to her daughter while she was incarcerated, similar scenarios play out in hundreds of homes every week. Indeed, Loren-Maltese has joined the fastest growing segment of the U.S. prison population: women with children under 18.

Remember, reporters have to tell a story. Help them to do their jobs. Give them sensory images that they and, therefore, their readers will not easily forget.

It's not that you can't ever use statistics or intellectual concepts, just remember that abstractions put people in their heads. They need to be in their hearts *and* they need to feel they have come up with their own conclusions in order to be moved and persuaded. Nobody reacts well to being told what to feel or do.

I was listening to the *World View* program on National Public Radio when Judith McKai, a Senior Policy Advisor for the World Lung Foundation, was explaining why tobacco control was good for the wealth and the health of a nation. Why is it important to limit the growth of the tobacco industry? Judith gave concrete examples of the hidden costs of cigarette smoking. She talked of "fires all over the world" (one-third of all fires are caused by careless smoking), "de-forestation to cut down trees for tobacco", and "an amazing amount of garbage, simply billions to clean up the matches, cigarettes, packets and lighters thrown away every single day." Other people might have kept re-iterating the abstract, summary statement: "There are enormous costs". However, being specific made Judith's point more believable.

To make your cause come alive, let your audience take the journey with you. Put them in a scene where they can *see* something. Don't take your audience's role away.

When you use Story Speak, you choose: When do you want your audience in their heads and when do you want them in their hearts? Being in the scene, in the movie, through sensory language is where emotions flow. The feelings are what attach people to your organization and your cause.

With thoughtful consideration you can make your story say exactly what you want it to say. Think of that! It's no small deal. Language is sometimes taken for granted. Just remember those times when you couldn't find the words, couldn't get your point across. As Mark Twain said, "The difference between the right word and the wrong word is the difference between lightning and a lightning bug." It's worth the effort and the time to find just the right word.

CHAPTER SIX
GETTING OTHERS TO SPEAK IN STORY LANGUAGE

What about getting other people to talk in Story Speak?

I know a lot of you get your articles for your newsletters, annual reports, and so on by interviewing your clients, your Board members, your donors, and your volunteers. Before hearing of Story Speak, you might have asked them a question such as, "Why do you think our organization is so important that you volunteer your time?" Think about it: you've asked them to give you an opinion and that's just what you'll get.

They'll answer back with an abstract comment such as "XYZ organization is important to our community."

That kind of testimonial might be influential, depending upon who the person is. But it's rarely memorable. Now, when you interview others, I want you to look for stories. And *you can only get stories by asking story questions*. Story questions evoke Story Speak.

You will ask, "Do you remember a time when…?" or "Was there ever a day when…? " "Tell me a story about a moment when…?"

First, get them to their answer in a time and place. Then, ask them all sorts of sensory questions. "What did your brother look like?" "Could you draw me a layout of the house? Where was that stairwell?" "Do you remember some of the sounds in the school hallways?" "What was a typical afternoon? What did you do?" "Where were you sitting?"

Specific sensory questions will give you descriptive and useable sensory answers. You will have people go through the same two-column process that you go through when creating stories: change summary statements into sensory details.

Let's say you are telling a story about a client of yours, a woman, who has overcome homelessness. Now, first of all, I've got to tell you that most people you interview don't think they have a story. They don't think there's anything interesting about their lives.

The person you are interviewing, for instance, might think there is nothing interesting about the fact that she was homeless and is now volunteering at your site or dancing in your troupe. It's typical for people to minimize their lives because they are so familiar with them. The barriers they've overcome don't even seem like achievements to them. It's just what they do or what had to be done.

The woman you're interviewing will say summary opinions such as, "Oh, yes. It was rough out there." And "Oh, yeah. It was cold out there, but my mother never wanted to go into the shelter".

Anyone seeing a movie yet? Actually your brain will try. When the person you're interviewing isn't giving you details, your mind will start to fill in by using the few images you already have about homelessness. But those might not be accurate. The person that you're interviewing hasn't told you his or her story yet.

Don't be frustrated or daunted when the person you're interviewing talks in large concepts and abstractions. Instead, start asking very specific sensory questions: "So let me see if I have this right. You'd be sleeping outside, even if it were 10 to 20 degrees out, using something like rags inside your clothing for insulation, and making a shelter out of old cardboard boxes. Is that right?"

It doesn't even matter if you have the wrong picture because they will likely correct you. "No! No! I never used cardboard boxes. I always found the best materials, like corrugated tin and canvas, and leaned them up against the steel garbage bins in the alleys. That would really block the wind."

You see, it doesn't matter if you are giving the wrong images (within reason – you don't want to come across as if you aren't listening). By talking specifically, you make the person you are interviewing talk back to you specifically – in sensory images.

Here's another example. Let's say you are coaching one of your volunteers to talk to other volunteers. You want this volunteer to talk about when he first had the desire to work with your organization. You ask about his childhood to try and find out when he was first lit up by the idea of service. You might ask, "How did you get involved in volunteering?" People will respond with vague, abstract statements at first, such as, "Oh! I've always been involved."

Do you see? There's no movie yet. But don't worry. You just ask, "Well, what kind of volunteering did you do when you were younger?"

"Oh, you know, I went out with my mother"

"Oh, so your mother was a volunteer! What kinds of things did she do?"

And they'll be vague again, and answer, "All kinds of things."

This is how adults talk! But hang in there; be patient. Eventually, you'll get a nugget such as, "Oh, she was a Red Cross volunteer. She worked for the Blood Bank."

"Ah! So you went out with her when she worked at the Blood Bank?"

"Yes."

(Don't get frustrated. Keep asking specific questions.) "How old were you?"

"Seven."

More concrete, yes? Keep asking specific, sensory questions: "What kind of kid were you? Were you kind of small for your age? Were you quiet?"

"Oh no! I was this big, lanky, clumsy thing. I was into everything. I sort of loped about."

"Well, what did you do to help? Did you just watch her, or did you actually have a job?"

"Oh! I had a job. I put out the drinks and cookies."

Ah! So now I have - volunteering for the Red Cross, working at the Blood Bank, seven years old, tall lanky kid! Starting to see a movie, aren't you? In the film trade, they call these details - "the establishing shot", the long shot, or series of images that gets us into the story.

So I'd keep asking, "Did people lie down, or were they sitting in chairs? How many people came at a time? Did they wait in line?"

All the time, I'm getting the setting for the story clearer. If I just asked, "What was the Blood Bank like?" I'd get an answer such as, "Nice." Instead, I ask, "When you offered drinks and cookies to the people, what exactly did you serve?"

"Oh, we always had orange juice and Salerno butter cookies."

Boom! I don't know about you, but when I hear orange juice and Salerno butter cookies, I am there. I'm in the scene now. It's specific. I'm getting pictures. The movie is running.

And then I can start asking other questions. He said he was a big lanky kid, and into everything. "Did you ever spill anything? Did anybody ever refuse the orange juice and cookies, and get woozy? Did anyone ever faint after they stood up? How were the old timers, those who came in regularly? How were they different from the 'newbies' who were, maybe, nervous about giving blood for the first time? Did you ever refuse anyone who volunteered to give blood? Why?"

I'm still getting visual and sensory details, but I'm also starting to look for some story conflict, right? We'll talk about this more in our fourth S – Story Structure – but a story is about a mess, a turning point, and a solution.

Some possible story "messes" for this man you're interviewing might be the day, as a seven year old, when he spilled all the orange juice. Or the day people in line began to complain, or someone was turned away and a shoving match erupted. Or the day someone fainted. It doesn't have to be earth-shattering conflict, but something has to *happen* to make a story. There has to be events to have a story, and those events need to be clearly depicted just as the setting and main characters are pictured.

After you've mined the interviewee's experiences for these golden nuggets, you'd coach your volunteer to pick different parts of this story to tell. You'll help him to *select and shape* the story depending on his Story Setup – his particular audience, objective, and format.

Out of all the images and stories you uncover, you might discover two parallel moments for this man, for example, between an experience he had as a young boy and the experiences he's having now while volunteering for your organization.

Or, for example, maybe you discover that this man became really selfish as he got older. He lost all that giving spirit that his mother had modeled for him. He was a workaholic; he was tied to his desk. His wife divorced him, and he became bitter about his losses. He realized that the spirit in his life had left him. But, then, on a whim – how that happened will be part of the story – he started volunteering at your organization and something changed in his life.

He realized how blessed he was. He rediscovered other talents and skills that he had, and how to laugh and care about others besides himself. Now you're creating a mini-movie that your audience can see and can identify with. Most everyone has felt lost at some point in their lives and, if they're lucky, have experienced times of rejuvenation. Why not have your organization associated with that universal, positive experience of rebirth?

Sensory description is an important aspect of Story Speak, but wait... there's more! Another aspect of Story Language is the use of metaphors and comparisons.

CHAPTER SEVEN
METAPHORS AND COMPARISONS

Story Speak is also metaphorical.

For instance, in thinking about that Blood Bank example just covered, blood might become a central metaphor for this volunteer's story. Blood is basic to survival, information is basic to a community's survival, and that's what your organization does. You pump survival into the community by delivering information just when people need it.

You have to watch that you don't overdo these metaphors, but it can create a word picture and a message in a very short amount of time.

One of my Foundation clients, the Evanston Community Foundation, calls themselves the city's "non-profit hub" and "the reservoir for community ideas."

Community Media Workshop, the organization that helps Nonprofits get more press attention (and where I first started teaching *Story Power for Nonprofit* seminars), uses: "We're like the little league coach that gets smaller Nonprofits off the bench and into the big game."

Anyone with the reputation of being a great communicator uses metaphors. You will realize this, if you listen with Story Speak in mind. I heard an educator ask at a school board meeting, "Who wants to play Russian Roulette with our kids' education? That's what our system is doing, picking and choosing who gets educated and who doesn't." He is the kind of person that people listen to.

I remember talk show host, Oprah Winfrey, describing how she felt seeing a fleet of boats in the harbor outside Sydney, Australia. Her name with a giant "O" was printed on each sail, done as a way to welcome her to Australia. Watch how the regatta becomes not only a real-life description, but also a metaphor for telling her audience to never give up hope:

> *"I was born in Mississippi on a dirt road. I couldn't find my name on a keychain or a lunch box. But God was saying to me, 'Don't worry 'bout no lunch box. There's a regatta in Sydney with your name on it.' And that's because of the grace from a Higher Power. Wherever you are and whatever you're doing, don't ever forget there's a regatta somewhere with your name on it."*

(Also notice how specific she was in the first sentence. She didn't say, vaguely, "I was born in a small town and I had an unusual name, so I didn't see it too often." No. She places us in Mississippi on a dirt road. Without her saying the word "poor", she's *shown* that she came from humble beginnings. She gives a quick idea of what it was like to search for her name on a keychain or lunch box – very concrete.)

Sometimes you just don't have time for a whole story, but you always have time for a quick comparison. In talking about what their renovated theater and office space building looked like before restoration, Virginia ("Ginny") Louloudes of the Alliance of Resident Theatres in New York said, "When we first looked at the building, every room was filled with cabinets, boxes, and broken furniture. It was like visiting an elderly relative who had once lived in a grand space but, now, all of it had fallen into disrepair."

That quick comparison made me feel as though I quickly understood what the Alliance had faced in renovating the building. Using more Story Speak, Ginny went on to describe the now "open floor plan, the light blue French Provincial style and the architectural forms such as arched doorways, crown molding and chandeliers that the Alliance made visible once again".

In showing (not telling) about the Alliance's purpose to provide small theater companies with office and meeting space, Ginny contrasts the isolation small theaters often experience with the theaters' unfamiliar dilemma in their new shared space. She gave a clear, descriptive example: "When you go to washroom, you have to decide sometimes how much time you're going to spend there. You'll often meet up with someone from another theater, and start sharing what you're doing and swapping ideas. All of a sudden, you realize thirty minutes have gone by. In the rest rooms, the halls, the lobby – it's like having several important mini-lunch dates without even having to set them up."

Quick, contrasting word pictures can be a great way to talk to your audience when you don't have much time or space, or if a news reporter wants only a brief comment for a radio spot or online blog.

Just the other day, I heard someone explaining the complicated 2008 economic recession brought on by the downfall in the housing market. The financial expert threw out a bunch of statistics about how relatively small the mortgage market was and of how an even smaller piece of the action could be attributed to sub-prime mortgages.

Some of you relate to numbers. One-half of ten percent of this or that is all you need to hear. For a lot of us, numbers mean little. They don't stick. This expert probably consciously or instinctively knew this and went on to give this analogy, saying, "That's like saying the rubber band factories in the United States went out of business and brought the entire U.S. economy down."

That was a great comparison! To me, it really drove home his point much better than statistics or making some bland statement such as, "The sub-prime mortgage sector is only a small part of the overall housing market."

Plus, this comparison moved me to participate. It made me ask the obvious question: "How could such a relatively small part of the economy have such a large effect?" It set me up for the rest of the expert's report, which explained how derivatives were bundled and parts of loans sold off and attached to other loans and so forth. Yes, these packages were a small part of the economy but they were attached to everything else. Comparisons and metaphors are such quick and effective ways to make complicated issues easier to understand.

Here are a couple of environmental examples:

- Instead of only talking about lead content as parts per million, an environmental group made a poignant comparison, "That's like having two, 1-pound bags of toxic lead dumped into your children's lungs every day."

- In talking about the flooding on the Mississippi River, an interviewee on the radio said, "The Mississippi is like a rowdy uncle - dispensing all kinds of goodies during good times, breaking the furniture during bad." Wow! That got my attention!

If I asked you about your favorite professors or teachers over the years, I bet at some point you would tell me they made things understandable – that they made you feel smart or at least hopeful that you would understand the concepts you were studying.

If a teacher was "clear" and "good at explaining things," they most likely used analogies, comparisons, and metaphors. "Israel is the size of Rhode Island" or "Americans throw away enough garbage every day to fill 63,000 garbage trucks, which if lined up end to end would stretch half way to the moon."

Suddenly, you have it! The concept is easily understood.

Maybe you're doing the fundraising for your organization and you don't have time during a radio program for a whole story. However, you do have time to say something such as, *"If just 95 people gave up just 1 cup of coffee for one day, just one day, that money would pay for every child in our school to be fed for the whole year."*

When you use a comparison, you're not simply throwing out an abstract number. You're quickly creating a picture in the mind of your audience. Use comparisons to let your donors know how little they have to sacrifice and how large their impact will be when they do. Help them to think, "My small sacrifice seems real and doable, the results tangible. I feel pride just imagining it."

Here's another example from the Jane Addams Senior Caucus, an advocacy group for seniors on the north side of Chicago. They were giving a talk with visual slides. One read: "Our state has invested more money in the horse racing industry than programs to help the elderly and working poor get affordable housing. Horses get $36 million; people get only $25 million."

The presenters didn't have to go on a rant. They made their point, quickly and concisely through the use of a clear comparison. "Sound bites" are not a new phenomena. People have been transmitting "sound bites" — little capsules of meaning - for thousands of years in the form of proverbs!

People all over the world have used proverbs because they are quick, astute comparisons. Proverbs give meaning without needing any elaborate explanations. They are specific and so they pack lots of wisdom in very short phrases because they create simple word pictures.

For example, at the same Jane Addams Senior Caucus, one of the seniors was talking to a reporter about why he didn't want to leave senior housing. The city had plans to tear down the senior high rise where he lived. The man quoted a Russian proverb at the press conference, "A young tree, if uprooted, can be replanted. If an old tree is uprooted, it will die."

That very short proverb was quoted in the news reporter's article. The meaning was clear: The young might adjust to a change in locale, but our older citizens need roots - that's what they find in secure, senior housing.

I will bet that if you asked people who read the paper that morning what they remembered, most of them would forget all the facts they read and remember that picture of a tree and its need for roots. The brain works in pictures. Practice speaking metaphorically and you will pack a lot of meaning into a very short phrase or two.

Another important point: your audiences can interpret statistics and facts differently. You can make a statement such as, "The U.S. spends $680 billion on defense." Some are going to be think, "That's too much!" and others, "That's too little!"

If people are going to understand your statistics the way you hope they will, you have to wrap your facts and statistics in a clear context. Story is the context that puts you in control of the message people will receive.

Finally, another aspect of story speak is Dialogue. When I was a kid, I read a lot. I also remember skimming through all the descriptions to get to the white space where the dialog happened. Conversations are engaging because they allow outsiders to listen in to what people are saying. What could be better than that?

I am sure many of us have had the experience of driving a long distance alone. The drive eventually becomes tedious, even though you're listening to music or to the radio. Then, at another time, you make the same ride with a friend in the car and you talk the entire time. The time flies by. You can't believe you're already at your destination!

Dialogue connects us. Conversation is one of the greatest attention-holding devices we have as human beings. So pepper some of your stories with dialogue. It's another way to create that "you are there" feeling for your audience.

Even if you're printing a financial report and don't have time for a full story, you could add a sidebar quote from someone. You could scatter a few provocative quotes in the report that catches the attention of people, and breaks up all those numbers. Your audience can imagine themselves listening to the person who's talking, having a conversation with them, and then believing the quote because a "real person" said it.

As you choose your words, your Story Speak, keep your audience and format in mind. You're going to get tired of hearing me talk about Story Setup, but it's not only the starting point; it also weaves into every aspect of a story. Your audience, your objective and your format – where you're telling your story – will determine much about the language you use.

For example, your website is more permanent and should, perhaps, be more formal, relatively speaking. Sometimes, it's your first exposure to your audience. Perhaps, it needs to be more official in tone because you haven't established a relationship with this newcomer to your organization yet.

View your language from your audience's point of view, not what makes sense or feels familiar to you. For example, choose descriptions, metaphors and comparisons that make sense to your audience. Your "in-house" language and frames of reference may mean nothing to the public. It's another part of having a marketing mindset.

Your online blog or other social media outlets, on the other hand, can be more informal. You can use more "in-house" language (although, still take time to give a quick definition for less unfamiliar terms). In fact, social media sites *need* personality or a way to give a "face" to your organization.

Keep your Story Setup in mind as you work with the three main tools of Story Speak:

1. specific, sensory descriptions
2. imagery, metaphors, proverbs and comparisons
3. dialogue and quotes

Target your story language within the spoken and unspoken agreements you have with your audience about how formal or informal you can be. Use Story Speak, and your stories will come alive and last in the mind of your audience long after the story has been told.

PART THREE
THE THIRD S:
STORY SETTING

CHAPTER EIGHT
A PARTICULAR TIME AND PLACE

Here's the definition of a story one more time:

"You know it's a story when the audience you want to reach can picture _a particular time and place_..."

What's the first thing they picture? A particular time and place. Our third S is Story Setting.

It is paramount that your story is set in a time and place. Right away, that moves your anecdote or story out of the abstract. Already your story is better!

Think of going to the theater to see a play. As you take your seat, the usher hands you a program. You open that program. Whether you're at your child's school play or a Broadway production, the program will give you the time and place in which the play is happening: "Brooklyn 1968" or "A small cellar in a French bakery during WWII."

I've said this before and will say it again, nonprofits that are doing good work often launch into a laundry list of statistics, accomplishments, and all the people they've reached.. Whoa! Slow down. Give people a chance to connect with you. Give them a chance to settle in to a Story Setting.

Even at a conference or at a local City Council meeting, you can introduce yourself by saying, "Hi, I'm so-and-so with the so-and-so foundation. We're in that building on the corner of 5th and Main that used to be an automotive dealer. Now, in the fancy showroom that once displayed high-end Cadillacs, our organization feeds 300 people a day."

I promise you. You will not be forgotten. Every time people go by 5th and Main, they'll think of you because you have grounded them in a place very quickly. You aren't just some abstract cause; you are real people working in a real place. Plus, you gave them two contrasting pictures – Cadillacs and soup kitchens. People, as I said in the last section, think in pictures, so you're making your communication memorable.

Everyone has probably experienced hearing a child tell a story, Little ones dive right into the story! "And then this happened… and then this happened… and then…", You have to say to the child, "Wait a minute! Let's start at the beginning. Where were you? When did this happen?" You are lost until you get grounded in time and place.

There's a reason why all the old stories begin, "Once upon a time, in a kingdom far, far, away…" The first sentence sets the story in a time and place. Think of your story as if it takes place on a stage. Describe the scenery. What does it look like? What am I seeing or hearing? Where *are* we?

Most of the time, unless you're doing a full-length story with many scenes or changes of scenery, your story is going to be a one-act play, You're going to be talking about one or two moments or days, in one or two places. No matter the length of your story, always ground people in a specific time and place first. A specific time and place *suggests a feeling* for your story right from the start.

I was working with a client, a very talented comedienne and speaker named Elaine on a talk she was going to give to college students about eating disorders. Describing her own struggle with anorexia and bulimia, she says, "Finally, in my last year of college, I confessed to my roommate that I had an eating disorder."

During our coaching call, I asked her to tell me, "Where were you when you 'confessed' to her? What were you doing? What was she doing?" In other words, I was asking her to set the scene.

This is an important moment, the moment Elaine finally shares with another human being that she has a problem. It will be much more dramatic if she sets the scene rather than tell *about* the moment. If we can be *in* the scene with her, we can feel something. Is Elaine looking at the floor as she speaks? Is she sitting on the coach and hugging a pillow to her chest? Does her roommate come and give her a hug or does she scrunch her face up in disgust?

If Elaine will describe that confessional moment in sensory detail, we will participate and, therefore, we will feel. If she tells us she said, "I have bulimia" into the pillow, in fact, Elaine's voice was so muffled that her roommate had to ask three times, "What did you say?", we will be *seeing* that she was ashamed. If Elaine doesn't use abstract nouns to tell us how she feels, but, instead, paints the scene, we are involved interjecting our own meaning and drawing our own conclusions.

If her roommate comes forward and gives her a hug and Elaine describes how she had "never sunk into such a soft sweater – to this day I love soft, blue sweaters", we know she's going to be okay. But if her roommate turns her back on Elaine and starts loading the dishwasher, we'll make an entirely different conclusion and even worry for Elaine.

Bring your audience into a time and place, so that they can see the events that unfold through your point of view. Elaine is inviting her audiences to break through the wall of silence and shame and so we need to be with her in the moment and in the place where she first speaks her truth. It's much more powerful to create a setting so that your audience joins you in your story rather than to tell your audience what they should think or do.

PART FOUR
THE FOURTH S:
STORY STAR

SUSAN O'HALLORAN

CHAPTER NINE
A PERSON WE CARE ABOUT

Our fourth S covers what many think of when considering a story - the main character. To keep the S alliteration going, we're calling this main character the Star of your story. The Star gets the story moving and keeps it moving. Plot is nothing more than the main character in action. He or she is the one we follow throughout the story.

"You know it's a story when your audience can picture *someone they care about..."*

A story is about a specific person. Yes, it can sometimes be about a group or a cause but, most of the time, it is best personified in *one person's* story. Mother Teresa said, "If I look at the mass, I will never act. If I look at the one, I will."

There was an interesting study several years ago, in 2004, by Carnegie Mellon University that showed this statement to be true. The researchers sent out two versions of a request letter for money. The first one had statistics on the magnitude of problems facing children in Africa – drought, food shortages, and displacement of people from their homes, and on and on.

The second version told *one* child's story, and talked about how the donated money would be used to feed her and send her to school. You can probably guess the outcome.

Yes, the second letter raised more money – twice as much money!

People reacted to the first statistics with what I call "the drop in the bucket effect." They experienced Compassion Fatigue. The factual evidence of massive suffering overwhelmed people. However, the second letter made people think, "I can do something." Remember Mother Teresa's words, "If I look at the mass, I will never act. If I look at the one, I will."

When you write or tell your story, give people a specific person to care about. Present your cause's challenges on a human level. For example, an organization that wants to show the ripple effect of losing smaller farms might tell the story of a single mother who works at the Main Street Diner. What happens if she loses her job because Main Street is turning into a ghost town as the large conglomerates gobble up more and more small farms, and the diner's clientele move away?

When it comes to the Specific Person in a story, consider using *yourself* as the Star of some of the stories you tell. You may be shy about being the center of your stories, or you may feel that your life just isn't that exciting. But it's precisely because you are a real human being that your audience will relate to you. Having *you* be part of the story can make a difference in how much your audience gets involved. It's actually the fastest way to build connection and credibility.

Why are you involved in your cause? Who got you involved? Telling the story of the person who got you so engaged in your organization's mission is a way to say a lot about the values of your program, and about why your work is so inspiring.

Other ways to effectively showcase your program through your personal stories include talking about what you cared about as a child, the things that made you sad or angry as you were growing up. When you talk about your values through a childhood story, the audience draws the parallel: "Well, if she or he cares about those values and they're involved in such and such organization… then that nonprofit must have those values, too." The audience, then, becomes a participant in piecing together your story.

Tell the story about a time everything changed, when you saw the world differently and so, suddenly, the mission of your organization became a prominent part of your life. Think about how many books or movies are sold because the plot is about a turning point in someone's life. Well, you've had turning points as well.

Find those moments when something jolts you off the complacency path you have been traveling into something new and meaningful. There's drama there, even if you don't think of your life that way. Those are the moments other people will identify with and, therefore, will build a connection with you and your organization.

I was teaching a seminar in Michigan and was chatting with a woman during the break who worked with parents and children. I asked her how she got started in foster care work and teaching parenting classes. She told me she had previously been a realtor, and she was showing an apartment one day. She had stopped by the building to make sure the house was in order before showing it. When she turned the key and opened the front door, she heard the television on. "That's odd," she thought. "The owner had said she wouldn't be a home for several days."

The woman walked to the back of the house where the kitchen was. There, sitting at the kitchen table watching the morning talk show, was a three-year-old boy. He sat in overpowering dirty diapers, licking his fingers as he ate from an almost empty jar of peanut butter. The woman discovered that the young boy had been dropped off by his addicted mother for her friend to "baby sit". The mother, in her drug-induced state, failed to notice that her friend wasn't even home. The boy had been alone to fend for himself for three days by the time the realtor found him.

This was the first non-biological child the realtor took into her own home. Now, as director of a parenting education agency, she has raised fourteen children in addition to her own biological child.

I asked this woman, "Where are you telling this story?" She answered innocently, "Oh, I don't think anyone would be very interested in what's happened to me. I just want to learn to talk about what the organization does."

Everyone does this. We take our accomplishments, experiences, and sacrifices for granted. If you heard that the director of the parenting organization had raised fourteen successful foster children of her own, would that not buy some instant credibility? I know I was immediately impressed by the heart of this woman, and was ready to hear anything she wanted to tell me about raising children.

To create a bridge or connection to your organization, go back to your Story Setup. Reflect on the audience you want to reach and ask, "What part of my life matches something they care about or a problem they're facing?"

Again, your stories don't have to be about life and death moments. You can tell stories about your first day on the job, or about how your family and friends react to your work. There might be some funny or very moving stories in seemingly simply everyday topics.

Think about what attracted you to your organization's mission in the first place. Even think about who disagreed with you. What obstacles did you have to face to get where you are now? Is there a client you have worried about - one you can't stop thinking about, even when you're on vacation? As you talk about that person, your audience will learn a lot about you, and by association, your organization.

If you think about how I started this book, I didn't give tons of credentials - not about where I went to school, or that I won this or that award. No, what I told you about is my Grandpa, the person who showed me the power of storytelling.

First of all, maybe there was some connection for you because you loved your grandfather, too, or wish you had a grandpa who told stories. Maybe you related to the memory and the humor as I was describing my city block on a summer night with everybody clipping their postage stamp size lawns and washing down their sidewalks. It was personal, right? And, really, that was more important in gaining credibility than if I had given you a hundred professional credentials.

When you think about it, who has influenced you? There's a saying: Do you feel connected because someone influenced you *or* did he or she influence you because you felt connected?

The thing about stories is they have what author, Annette Simmons, calls a *pull* rather than a *push* strategy. Sometimes you can push people to do things, but that interaction is more related to the sleazy sales model we want to avoid. Pushing people can make them do things, but it can also make them want to push back.

A pull strategy such as storytelling brings people in… pulls them in. And, then, they're likely to stay there.

Listen to this story from Jill of Heartland Community College in Normal, Illinois when I was working with her in 2012:

"A few years ago when President Obama was our state Senator, our students actually wrote letters to him telling him what our college program meant to them and how it was changing their lives. I hand delivered those letters to him when he was our Senator. To know that the now President has heard the voices of our students is pretty amazing."

There's a story in there, yes? First, Jill would need to get clear on her story's Setup. What's the point of telling this story? What does she want to accomplish? Who's her audience? If she were speaking to a group of angry voters, she'd pitch the story differently than if she were speaking to a group of President Obama supporters.

What's the format for the story – where will the audience be? How much time does Jill have to tell her story? Even if the organizers of a community event tell Jill she has 20 minutes to present, if, for instance, she discovered that there would a band and a fundraising auction down the hall, she might want to prepare a 10 minute and a 15 minute version of her presentation. Take the time to get every bit of the Setup right.

Next, Jill would want to fill in the details of the story by asking herself: "What were in some of those letters? What did the room where we met look like? What did Senator Obama look like on that day? What did he say? How did he react to the letters from your students?"

Rather than an abstract, overarching feeling "It was so nice to meet him", Jill would work to draw out images that would *show* how she felt. Was her hand sweaty as she shook the President's hand, or did she sit in a leather chair and feel her back relax into it? Then, *the audience* could participate in story - listening to Jill, but running a little mental commentary, drawing conclusions and becoming part of the scene: "Oh, she was surprisingly calm. He put her at ease right away. Oh, that's how I'd be…" and so forth.

Don't be afraid to tell stories where you are the main character. It's precisely because Jill is in the story and she's the one standing in front of her audience that the story is so engaging and believable.

Second, by listening in on what Jill and the students said to then Senator Obama, the audience will hear indirectly all kinds of values and benefits of Heartland Community College's programs.

If Jill structures the story so that there is some drama - for example, if one of her students is too nervous to talk but is a huge fan of Obama's — then she can lace in all kinds of information about her programs while we watch this student struggle to find his voice. It won't feel as if Jill is bragging or forcing an opinion on the audience. If she can make people care about this student and put him in a bit of a situation, then it will be easy for the audience to get caught up in how the story will end.

Think of how many times you have given money or your time because you liked the person who asked you to get involved. A few months back, I was volunteering at a bike-a-thon for an environmental group and some friends asked me, "You've been so busy lately. Why did you give up a Saturday?"

And I said, "Yeah, it's crunch time in my business right now, but the guy who asked me is really a nice guy..."

Yes, I cared about the cause we were raising money for that day, but the truth is... I care about a lot of causes. I gave up a Saturday for him because I like him, because I knew the bike-a-thon was important to *him*. Just because you're the storyteller doesn't mean you can't be in the story. Your personal experience and motivation can help people connect to why they should take an interest and get involved in your organization.

When it comes to creating a Star or Specific Person, let's talk about what it means to "care about" them. Maybe it's not essential that your audience fall in love with your story's main character, but your audience does need to identify with or, at the very least, be curious about him or her.

Next, you must be clear on what the main character wants and, therefore, what's at stake in this story. If some crucial college funding is at stake, then it matters to us how Senator Obama receives Jill's message. Or if Jill tells the story from the shy student's point of view and shows the hardships he is facing then, miracle of miracle, this student rises to full stature and addresses his political representative with power and passion, then that student's victory becomes a community victory. We've just *experienced* the college's mission of sending confident young citizens into the world,

Most of the time, you are going to focus on one specific person who is the Star of your story — if for no other reason than it takes too long to describe the background information and challenges of several people. Yes, there are many popular TV shows with ensemble casts. However, these shows have months to develop each character's story.

Still, there are times when you are going to want or need to make a whole group of people – all the clients you serve - come alive at once and quickly. For example, when I was giving a presentation about how adult education changes lives, I said, "Adult education touches a diversity of adult learners - from the person letting go of the shame and barriers of illiteracy to the immigrant starting a new life, from the young person who had to leave high school to look after an ill parent to the first generation high school graduate who hands his diploma to his son, modeling a pathway to college for his children…"

In a small amount of time and space, I shared several *types* of people that adult education serves. I gave each type of person a simple tag or marker that would make them distinct. This kind of group Star through quick images is like a movie montage.

You might not have the time to get to know each person, but you do have the sense that these are real people who faced real challenges. In addition, if I want to give statistics on how many people were reached despite cutbacks in funding, my audience is at least partially grounded in the context that this isn't just a bunch of numbers – real people's lives are being affected here.

So, to be clear: I am not saying that every story has to be about one person, but there should be a *human* element in every one of your stories.

It's interesting to me that national newspapers are all having trouble with circulation, but many small-town local newspapers are doing well. Why is that? Because they mention people by name, people the readers know and want to hear about. My father retired to a small community with a local paper. Every time I came to visit, people would say hello to me in the store and on the street. It took me awhile to catch on that people already knew that I was going to be there because they'd read the "Who's Visiting" column of the paper.

Facebook became a success because, in part, Mark Zuckerberg hit on a simple formula: people want to hear about people they know.

Studies show us that when babies are placed in front of close up photos or videos of people's faces, they squeal with delight. We are wired to relate to other people. You know when you get in that grocery checkout line, you find your eyes sneaking over to the tabloids even though you might not give one hoot about the gossip. You really don't care about popular culture, but it's almost impossible not to scan those headlines. As human beings, we are endlessly curious about each other.

Create characters that people like, care about, identify with or, at the very least, are curious about. That's what gets the story going.

How do movies begin? Right away, it introduces a Setting. The camera pans across gears and other machinery parts and eventually we recognize an abandoned factory as the location. We are somewhere.

Then, pretty quickly or you would become bored and frustrated, the main character (the Star of the film) appears. Do the same in your stories. Never confuse your audience with who the story is about.

PART FIVE
THE FIFTH S:
STORY STRUCTURE

SUSAN O'HALLORAN

CHAPTER TEN
FACING OBSTACLES

I know you've heard this before. But let's say it together again:

You know it's a story when...

The audience you want to reach can picture a certain time and place where someone they care about **faces greater and greater obstacles in trying to reach his or her goal.**

Five Story Elements have been identified so far:

❶ Story Setup – designing your story for the audience you want to reach and selecting the format you will use

❷ Story Speak – creating word pictures, metaphors and dialogue

❸ Story Setting – positioning your story in a certain time and place

❹ Story Star or Specific Person – presenting a main character about whom your audience cares or is curious

❺ And, finally, Story Structure – placing greater and greater obstacles in your Star's way before he or she can reach the goal

Remember, a story is a narrative or a sequence of events. What gets a story started is that there's a problem, a challenge, a mess to clean up, or a situation. It doesn't have to be earth shattering, but there does have to be *action*.

Something needs to be happening. A story is not a collection of ideas, themes, or even images. To make sure you are telling a story, ask yourself, "What is the situation or problem, and what happens next because of it?"

I remember a haunting image that a client of mine gave upon discovering the night before her marriage that her soon-to-be husband was HIV positive. The young man had been tortured for months by how to tell his fiancée that he had been unfaithful. As they lay in bed talking excitedly about their plans to start a family, he could continue the deception no longer. He blurted out his HIV status. The woman bolted out of bed and sat shell shocked in their living room. They had re-decorated, and the whole room had that new furniture and carpeting smell. Many wedding gifts had already arrived and were stacked on the dining room table, silhouetted in the moonlight like a boxy castle. She sat staring out at the streetlights until the sun rose and streaked golden rays onto the living room floor.

A great image, yes? But it's not a story… yet. There's definitely a mess. A situation. We've got an intriguing opening, but more is needed to be fully drawn into this woman's life, and her later involvement in HIV/AIDS education.

This image is a great Story Start or Story Hook. If she has only a short time to speak for HIV/AIDS education, giving this image would be a dramatic start to any "Why I Became Involved" presentation. But, if there's time and it fits her communication objective, she could give more details before this moment of disclosure. In a full-out story, she would let herself become a character in this story.

She could, for instance, share anything that is at stake, besides the obvious. Maybe this woman had sworn an oath never to love again. This relationship with her fiancée represents the slow healing of a heart that had been broken too many times. Maybe her father, her last remaining parent is dying and had always dreamed of seeing his youngest married. In a longer story, the characters and what's at stake for them would be further developed.

Also, in a longer story, something more would happen beyond the initial shock of her fiancée's news. How did she react? Did she call off the wedding? Whom did she tell? It's what your English teacher probably labeled as the beginning, the middle, and the end of a story. The same incident can be told as a thirty-second image to introduce your talk, or may become a ten-minute story that anchors a much longer presentation. Think of your stories as accordions that can shrink or expand, depending upon your Story Setup.

When your analysis shows the need for a full-out story, that's when you must pay special attention to and become skilled at Story Structure.

What would you think if you paid to see a movie in a theater and saw the opening scenery, followed by another beautiful opening shot, next a picture of a downtown street, and then a mountain view with nothing happening for the next 90 minutes?

You would feel like you were watching someone's vacation video, right? Would you sit and stare at those scenes for an hour and a half, though? Probably not. It's fine to have a DVD of a fire burning in a fireplace to stare at, but there's an unspoken agreement between the teller and the audience when a story of a longer format is told. It's the expectation that *something will happen* beyond a single image, regardless of how startling or evocative that image may be.

When you pay ten dollars or more to go to a movie, the characters must be relatable. They must also be doing something, facing something, and eventually transcending or learning from life's challenges. Something needs to happen.

You don't need to invent problems. Who hasn't experienced the challenges that life brings? While we can hope for some breaks in our lives, and periods of calm from time to time, the troubles of life don't suddenly go away. All you can expect from life is a better set of problems. You and your organization have plenty of difficulties from which you can create an endless stream of stories.

While challenges are the common thread in our lives, how they are approached depends upon whether they are seen as a breakdown or as an opportunity. All human beings face barriers and, as human beings, we are endlessly curious to see how others face their particular set of problems. That's why stories are so engaging.

For example, suppose that someone said they were going to tell a story about a time they thought they knew it all and then found out they didn't? Don't you immediately feel interested to know about the mistakes of others? Again, the story may not be about earth shattering, life-or-death moments. Simple, everyday moments of arrogance and, then, learned humility are one of those interesting potholes on the journey through life. People want to know how life's bumps and sharp curves are navigated by others. It's much more interesting than "Here's a time when everything went right."

Think, for example, of "before" and "after" stories that you can tell about your organization. Begin, for instance, by identifying your Star as a client you worked with and show us how he or she got involved with your group – that's the "before". By the end of the story, he or she ends up, most likely, in a good place that exemplifies the work of your organization – that's the "after".

But what happened in the middle? What barriers did the character have to get past? When did things go wrong? When did things look bleak? Who else is affected by these problems? What would it have meant if he or she didn't succeed? Where's the "mess"? Where's the turning point? What was learned?

That's what structure is all about – plot out each scene that shows the Star moving toward and away from his or her goal. If you set it up right, the audience wants to know how things turn out. When listening to a story on the radio that's so intriguing that you can't turn it off, ask yourself: Why can't I leave this story? What is it I *have* to know?

When thinking about structure for your organization's stories, ask yourself, "Was there a time something went wrong, or a time our program was tested?" As long as you have a successful "after" story to tell, admitting your mistakes as learnings will actually give people more confidence in your group. The fact that you went through challenges builds a connection with your audience. The fact that you came through the challenges wiser and better than ever builds trust.

And remember, some of these stories should be about you.
When did you fall short of how you wished you could be? When
was a time you dressed wrong for the job? Or the day you got
locked out, or forgot an appointment? When did you laugh on the
job and you shouldn't have? While you are telling funny stories
about your misfortunes, you can be sharing all kinds of great
things about your organization's values and mission.

CHAPTER ELEVEN
THE STORY START

Let's start at the beginning of Story Structure. How you structure the start of your story is crucial to grabbing the audience's interest.

Start as close to the situation or problem as possible. The phrase I like to use is "Get in late.". In other words, don't give miles of background information. Everyone knows people who do this - those who give so much background information that you're tempted to interrupt them and ask, "And the point is?" They are giving you so much detail it's not at all clear what you should focus on or why you should care. It's only the beginning of the story, and you're already lost.

Start your story with a strong Story Hook. The Story Start or Hook needs to have an "Uh-oh" factor. Present a situation that makes the audience think, "Uh-oh. Trouble's coming!" and they'll stick around to see how things turn out.

Soon after, let the audience know what the Star wants and what it means if he or she doesn't get it. What's at stake? This is the important "So what?" dynamic. Something has to be at stake for the audience to care. Everyone needs a job, but if the sheriff is coming next month to kick you and your family out of your apartment - now that job *really* means something.

Again, the "something at stake" doesn't have to be life and death such as "If the scientists don't find the antibody, the planet and every human being on it will die in 48 hours." (Notice how common these types of movies are even though they have a predictable ending. When something important is at stake, we will keep watching.).

However, think of and share what finding a solution to the problem *means* to the Star of your story. For example, perhaps, your Star wants to succeed in your organization's program to show her immigrant father that all his sacrifices to bring his family to America were worth it.

Or maybe a child has a disability and only feels that she belongs when she's singing in your children's choir.

Or, perhaps, after your organization presented a theater piece on sexual violence last year a dozen victims came forward to talk to your counselors. If you don't get the renewed funding for a similar tour this year, how many will stay in the shadows suffering in silence and missing out on the help you could provide?

Ask yourself, "What's at stake?"

Once I was working with an organization that wanted to tell about the importance of fixed rental units for senior citizens. Here is the beginning of the story they created. Notice how quickly the clear "Uh-oh" factor and "So what?" dynamic are presented.

What does a senior citizen do when she retires on a fixed income (her income is halved) and, then, her rent doubles? Where does she go if she has to move out?

The "Uh-oh" is that her rent doubles just as her income is cut in half. She's got a problem, yes? The "So what?" says that a lot is at stake, that she might not be able to afford to stay where she lives – "Where will she go?"

So many times we start our stories with the conclusion. We give away too much information too early. "Our housing counselors help seniors find affordable homes. Last year, we relocated two dozen seniors." You've done all the work. There's nothing for the audience to participate in.

Instead, give a Situation with a Story Hook that makes the audience care and ask, "Well, how did it turn out? What happened?" By holding back some information, you create Suspense. So a few more S's for you:

The Story Start begins close to a Situation (get in late) with an "Uh-oh!" factor (troubles coming) and a "So what?" dynamic (this is what it means if this mess isn't fixed), all the time holding back information to create Suspense.

Here is that same woman's full Story Start (after a little coaching):

> I was sitting in my kitchen last year, and I made myself a nice cup of peppermint tea.

(See the sensory language? Not a ton of detail – that would slow the story down, but a couple of nice details – kitchen and peppermint tea, and boom! She's given me the setting. I'm in a scene. I'm there and I believe her – it feels real.)

> I was sitting in my kitchen last year, and I made myself a nice cup of peppermint tea as I sat down to pay my bills. I had just retired after 30 years of working as a nurse's aide, and I wasn't worried about finances.

(By telling me she worked as a nurse's aide for thirty years, I get a feel for the kind of reliable, caring person she is. Even when the story is about you, you have to treat yourself like a character in the story; you have to take the time to let the audience get to know and like you. Then, as soon as she says, "I wasn't worried." We know there's something to worry about, don't we? We say to ourselves, "Uh-oh!")

I had planned well for my retirement. I was prepared to live on half of my usual income. So I was setting each bill aside – no surprises – and, then, I opened a letter from my landlord and almost choked on my tea!

(Do you see how that is better than telling the audience – "I was shocked! I couldn't believe it!" We, as the audience, have to work a little here. She tells us she about *choked on her tea* and I'm left to conclude – "Uh-oh, trouble! And wonder, "What's in the letter?")

…I opened the letter and there was a note saying my rent was going to double! My income was half of what it used to be, and now my rent was going to double? I couldn't afford a double rent payment every month! What was I going to do? Would I have to leave the home that I loved? Where would I live?

(The "So what?" dynamic – we know what's at stake right from the beginning).

She asks the question, and we're left to wonder the same thing. "What *is* she going to do?" and we're identifying, "What would I do?" We've got ourselves a situation here where something is at stake.

Create stories that hold back information in order to plant the question, "What happened next?" in the mind of your audience, and the story will keep moving forward. Plus, the obstacles you select to include in the story will give you a chance to showcase other solutions your organization offers and the compassion and skill of your staff.

CHAPTER TWELVE
RISING AND FALLING ACTION

What keeps a story compelling is the rising and falling of the action. The rise in action is the Star moving toward his or her goal. The fall in action is the Star moving away from his or her goal. You want to add complications to the original problem and the attempted solutions. As the storyteller, *you* structure or plot where those rising and falling situations occur in the story.

To discover events for the falling action (the movement *away* from the goal) for the woman's story discussed in the last chapter, you might ask:

- Did you talk to your landlord? Was he or she open to negotiating?
- Were other tenants similarly shocked?
- When did you think things looked most hopeless?
- When did you think – this is it, I'll never make it?
- What other times in your life have you been this financially afraid?

Rising action (the movement *toward* the goal) for the same story might include asking questions such as:

- Who offered hope?
- Who came forward to help? What did they do for you?
- What beliefs about yourself did you have to challenge to face this situation?
- At what moment did you think, "Maybe this will work out after all?"

Seesawing the action creates suspense. Some have called this way of plotting a story the "So/But Formula".

"Somebody wanted this, but this happened, so they did this. Oh, but this happened. So they did this. But, oh. my gosh, this happened."

"So… but… so… but…" You seesaw your Star back and forth, back and forth, toward and away from what he or she wants. This kind of seesawing back and forth is delightful to our brains. We are wired to respond positively to this seesaw story structure after years of listening to and watching stories.

Best of all, this seesaw action creates empathy. The listening or reading audience will love your group or organization because they vicariously experienced some of what this woman experienced. They feel grateful to your organization for relieving *their* tension. Your audience will get, really get, what it is that you do and what that *means* to people because they have a visceral feeling of what it would mean to them.

You already have all kinds of stories. You just want to more consciously use Story Structure to give a good Story Start. Then, with rising and falling Seesawing action, create even more Story Suspense.

Ready for more S's?

Story Structure consists of a Situation introduced by a Story Start or Hook (the "Uh-oh" and "So what?"). Then, it creates and prolongs Suspense though Seesawing back and forth, toward and away from the main character's goal until there's a Seminal Moment or turning point. There's a moment of Stillness, sometimes just a split second, where everything changes. You can almost read the Star's mind, "I'm not taking this anymore" or "This has gone far enough; I must act!" The Star *makes a decision*, does something (a climatic action), and a Solution is finally reached.

Again, Story Structure consists of:

- A Situation introduced by a Story Start followed by
- Seesawing action that creates Suspense until we reach
- A Seminal Moment, a moment of Stillness, a turning point where the Star makes a decision and climatic action follows
- A Solution, a resolution or an insight, is reached.

Interview your client (or yourself or whomever the story is about) for a bunch of "Uh-oh" moments or Situations. Then, arrange those situations. Begin with a great opening, a Story Start with Uh-Oh and So What? Factors, then arrange the Situations that will get the Star of your story in hot water. Continue by creating suspense for the audience - add more hot water, then scalding hot water – as this will cause the audience to ask, "What will happen next?"

About the end of your story… if you begin your story by "getting in late," you want to end your story with "getting out early."

What I mean by "Get out early" is, once you've told the story – end it! Get out! Everyone has heard someone tell a story and, then, tell it again. After that, just to make sure you understood the point, they tell you one more time what it all means. You want to structure your story to "Get out early!"- right after the resolution - so you don't have your audience screaming, "Alright already. We get it!"

Of course, there are other kinds of Story Structures in addition to someone moving toward and away from a goal in chronological time. You've heard or watched stories that begin with the ending. In these cases, the "after" story is told first. Then, the story fades to a series of flashbacks to show the background. How did we get to that "after" story?

Whatever form you use, make sure to consciously choose the structure of your story. You need to have some story buddies who will listen to or read your stories. Teach them what you now know about effective storytelling. Be clear with them about your Story Setup so they can give you helpful feedback.

Is the way you've structured the story having the desired effect?

Did you "get in late" and "get out early"?

Is your Star someone we care about, and is it clear what he or she wants?

Having an outside ear for your stories can really help you assess if you're reaching your communication goals. I never tell a story in public without first running it by my storytelling buddies. We're often too close to our own stories to see that our structure is sagging - we've missed an important piece of background information or an opportunity to prolong the suspense. Plus, getting feedback from trusted listeners will fuel your motivation to keep working on your stories. They do take work, you know ☺. But it's work you don't have to do alone.

CHAPTER THIRTEEN
PUTTING THE FIRST 5 S's TOGETHER

If you are going to be telling a longer story, you need full out Story Structure, Here is an example from one of my "Story Power for Nonprofits" seminars of a story used in a keynote presentation. First read the whole story and, then, see if you can identify the first 5 Story S's we've covered in the previous chapters. Then, I'll identify the elements of the story for you and explain their uses.

*

AUDIENCE: Financial professionals

COMMUNICATION GOAL: To inspire and motivate financial professionals to contribute financial support or in-kind donations to our financial literacy program

FORMAT: A 45-minute presentation. This story is key to asking them to get involved with our organization

PLACE: The financial group's association meeting after the annual luncheon

If you walk into my neighborhood hardware store, you might not notice 21-year-old Ricardo stacking shelves and sweeping floors. He's a tall kid, all legs and arms, with a sweet expression on his face. He has the brightest smile until you need something. And, then, his face scrunches in concentration. He turns into the professional. He's up a ladder to find you just the right screw, nut or bolt. You would never guess that just a few short years ago, Ricardo was living under the Wabash Street bridge, cardboard and blankets the walls of his house, rolled up rags the insulation for his clothes.

And you would never guess that even after all the help we were giving Ricardo in our program (including G.E.D. classes, living in a group home and finding a job), Ricardo almost wound up back on the streets because of an oversight, a hole in our program.

We were able to get Ricardo a job at a local restaurant, washing dishes. The first pay day Ricardo caught up with some of his buddies. They were all gathered around a fire in a garbage can warming themselves talking and laughing. He hadn't planned on it, but Ricardo found himself bragging that he had gotten paid. He doesn't know when it happened, but, by the time, he returned to the group home his paycheck which he had cashed into twenty dollar bills was gone.

With no adult in his life having steady employment what does Ricardo know? The whole world of commerce is a mystery to him. He's never had cash to even know he shouldn't be carrying it around.

But Ricardo did remember his grandmother telling him, "If you ever have money, Ricardo, you keep it where you are staying because if it burns down the man who owns the apartment has insurance. You get your money back."

So Ricardo proudly received his next paycheck, cashed it and stashed it in his closet at our group home. A section of plasterboard in the closet was loose. Ricardo pried the board open and stuffed his money in the wall. Well, lo and behold, the next day that money was missing, too!

All along Ricardo was finishing his GED. He also took one of our classes in interviewing. With coaching, Ricardo got up the nerve to apply for the hardware job. He was ecstatic when he landed it. He told us that he'd always loved to build things. Eventually, he was even teaching some classes on the floor of the store, demonstrating power tools, how to wallpaper and how to build toy chests for children. Eight months into the job, working with our partners, XYZ social service agency, Ricardo moved into his own apartment.

However, Ricardo spent the first nights in his apartment once again stuffing rags into his clothing to protect himself from the winter cold.

Ricardo didn't want to tell anybody. He was embarrassed. He thought it was his fault, that he'd done something wrong. He missed his first day of work ever because he hadn't slept all night.

It turned out there was no heat in the apartment, no electricity. We give our clients the information to turn on the utilities and we leave them be the first few days so that they can experience their independence. They know to call us. But Ricardo was too ashamed. When he called the utility companies, they told him they couldn't get him connected until he paid $250. The reason wasn't revealed until later. As Ricardo's mother moved the children in and out of homelessness, she had used a different child's name for the utilities each time she got an apartment. By the time he was 19 years old, Ricardo, unbeknownst to him, already had terrible credit.

Finally, Ricardo confided in us and our team was able to rectify the situation. The utility companies gave Ricardo a six-month probation period to clear his name.

Thanks to Ricardo and others, we realized that our training programs didn't go far enough. We hadn't taught our clients how to open checking and savings accounts, how to balance a check book, how to deal with utility companies and what could go wrong, for instance, how to check their credit rating.

The happy ending is that because of Ricardo's experience, we now have a financial literacy program and actually Ricardo, in addition to his hardware job, has come back as one of the facilitators in our program to teach other young people financial literacy.

CHAPTER FOURTEEN
THE FIRST FIVE S's IDENTIFIED

Here is our story's **SETUP**:

AUDIENCE: Financial professionals

COMMUNICATION GOAL: To inspire and motivate financial professionals to contribute financial support or in-kind donations to our financial literacy program

FORMAT: A 45-minute presentation. This story is key to asking them to get involved with our organization

PLACE: The financial group's association meeting after the annual luncheon

> *If you walk into my neighborhood hardware store, you might not notice 21-year-old Ricardo stacking shelves and sweeping floors. He's a tall kid, all legs and arms, with a sweet expression on his face. He has the brightest smile until you need something. And, then, his face scrunches in concentration. He turns into the professional. He's up a ladder to find you just the right screw, nut or bolt. You would never guess that just a few short years ago, Ricardo was living under the Wabash Street bridge, cardboard and blankets the walls of his house, rolled up rags the insulation for his clothes.*

Okay, I should have your attention. You should at least be curious. How did this young man go from homelessness to that job at the hardware store? Also, do you like this young man? I hope so. How did I make him likeable? (STORY STAR) I tell you right away that he has a job. Also, he helps people. He'll run up the ladder to get you just the right piece of hardware. In addition, I need to give a couple specific details to make you feel homelessness more than a word (**STORY SETTING** and **STORY SPEAK**). ("Living under the Wabash Street bridge, cardboard and blankets the walls of his house, rolled up rags the insulation for his clothes.")

Now I can create a double hook here. There's a hook about what happened to Ricardo, but I can also create a hook about the financial literacy program. (**STORY STRUCTURE – THE STORY HOOK**)

> *And you would never guess that even after all the help we were giving Ricardo in our program (including G.E.D. classes, living in a group home and finding a job), Ricardo almost wound up back on the streets because of an oversight, a hole in our program.*

Wait! A hole in our program? Do you see how it creates curiosity (**STORY STRUCTURE - SUSPENSE**)? I'm telling you that something went wrong, but I don't tell you what... yet. It's so important to hold back information. If I had used the "Tell 'em what you're going to tell them" formula, you wouldn't have to wonder about anything. I'd be doing all the work for you. Too many speakers "spill the beans" by telling us upfront in too much detail what they are going to speak about.

"Tell them what you're going to tell them/Tell them/Tell them what you just told them" may be clear communication for teaching certain concepts, but it's boring storytelling. Make them wonder. Make them guess! Hold back information.

"Ricardo almost wound up back on the streets because of an oversight, a hole in our program."

You see there is an "Uh-oh" factor – trouble's coming! There's also the "So What?" (**STORY STRUCTURE – STORY START**) We know what this means to Ricardo: If our organization doesn't get this right he's going to be back living under that bridge.

It's okay to admit that your organization had a blind spot because, of course, at the end, you're going to come through. Oddly enough, people will trust you even more because your success was hard won. You learned from your oversight.

So, I've got my Setting, my Star, my Story Structure, a couple of Hooks giving us some Suspense and, now, I start some up and down seesawing Structure.

> *We were able to get Ricardo a job at a local restaurant, washing dishes. The first pay day Ricardo caught up with some of his buddies. They were all gathered around a fire in a garbage can warming themselves talking and laughing. He hadn't planned on it, but Ricardo found himself bragging that he had gotten paid. He doesn't know when it happened, but, by the time, he returned to the group home his paycheck which he had cashed into twenty dollar bills was gone.*

His first payday represents an upswing. Ricardo is moving toward his goal of staying off the streets. His money being stolen – a definite downturn. (**STORY STRUCTURE – SEESAW**) He's moving away from his goal. Notice quickly that I've created a quick scene. Ricardo didn't just meet up with his buddies. They are standing around a lit garbage can warming themselves. Just one sentence, but instead of a concept, your audience has a short movie in their imaginations. (**STORY SPEAK**)

> *With no adult in his life having steady employment what does Ricardo know? The whole world of commerce is a mystery to him. He's never had cash to even know he shouldn't be carrying it around.*
>
> *But Ricardo did remember his grandmother telling him, "If you ever have money, Ricardo, you keep it where you are staying because if it burns down the man who owns the apartment has insurance. You get your money back."*
>
> *So Ricardo proudly received his next paycheck, cashed it and stashed it in his closet at our group home. A section of plasterboard in the closet was loose. Ricardo pried the board open and stuffed his money in the wall. Well, lo and behold, the next day that money was missing, too!*

I didn't give you the background of Ricardo's unfamiliarity with checking accounts and such or his grandmother's advice in the beginning of the story because it would have slowed the story down. You want to weave in background information sparingly through any story. Also, notice that a little bit of dialogue breaks up the narrative and gives the speaker a chance to add some variety to his or her voice. **(STORY SPEAK)**

In terms of structure, Ricardo receives another paycheck. He's living in a group home and off the streets – upswing. Then, even more money gets stolen – down turn. Ricardo is moving away from his goal.

All along Ricardo was finishing his GED. He also took one of our classes in interviewing. With coaching, Ricardo got up the nerve to apply for the hardware job. He was ecstatic when he landed it. He told us that he'd always loved to build things. Eventually, he was even teaching some classes on the floor of the store, demonstrating power tools, how to wallpaper and how to build toy chests for children. Eight months into the job, working with our partners, XYZ social service agency, Ricardo moved into his own apartment.

First, notice that I didn't simply say, "Ricardo did real well at the hardware store". It didn't take a long description, but mentioning power tools, wallpaper and toy chests gave you the chance to see Ricardo in action and conclude for yourself that he was doing well on this job and had a talent for it. **(STORY SPEAK)**

Plus, mentioning "toy chests for children" and other ways Ricardo was helpful keeps Ricardo's likeability factor going (**STORY STAR**). Mentioning one of your partners, a social service agency you work with, is always a good idea. You get credibility from their credibility. We are on a definite upswing.

> *However, Ricardo spent the first nights in his apartment once again stuffing rags into his clothing to protect himself from the winter cold.*

Aren't you wondering why? If I were coaching this speaker in presentation, this would be a place for a several seconds pause as the speaker wonders along with the audience.

> *Ricardo didn't want to tell anybody. He was embarrassed. He thought it was his fault, that he'd done something wrong. He missed his first day of work ever because he hadn't slept all night.*

Oh my! I'm dragging out the reveal, aren't I? Suspense doesn't have to be life and death situations. Just withhold information. Tease your audience a little bit. (**STORY STRUCTURE creating SUSPENSE**)

It turned out there was no heat in the apartment, no electricity. We give our clients the information to turn on the utilities and we leave them be the first few days so that they can experience their independence. They know to call us. But Ricardo was too ashamed. When he called the utility companies, they told him they couldn't get him connected until he paid $250. The reason wasn't revealed until later. As Ricardo's mother moved the children in and out of homelessness, she had used a different child's name for the utilities each time she got an apartment. By the time he was 19 years old, Ricardo, unbeknownst to him, already had terrible credit.

So it turns out that Ricardo already had a bad credit rating with the utilities companies. He can't get heat, water or electricity. This definitely represents a downswing and the most tragic of our three down swing events: buddies steal money, money stolen from the group home and, now, Ricardo freezing in his apartment. (Building **STORY STRUCTURE**)

Finally, Ricardo confided in us and our team was able to rectify the situation. The utility companies gave Ricardo a six-month probation period to clear his name.

Thanks to Ricardo and others, we realized that our training programs didn't go far enough. We hadn't taught our clients how to open checking and savings accounts, how to balance a check book, how to deal with utility companies and what could go wrong, for instance, how to check their credit rating.

The low point, the crisis point (**STORY STRUCTURE – SEESAW**) – poor Ricardo freezing in his apartment, starting to miss work – what seems to be the worst, turns out to be a good thing. The problem is resolved and insight for Ricardo and our program is gained.

This is Story Structure as old as the ages.

> *The happy ending is that because of Ricardo's experience, we now have a financial literacy program and actually Ricardo, in addition to his hardware job, has come back as one of the facilitators in our program to teach other young people financial literacy.*

If it were possible and you could bring Ricardo onto the stage at this point – that would be terrific. Or, at least, show photos of Ricardo at work in the hardware story, living happily in his apartment and working with other clients at your center.

After the story, you start to make your pitch. You sprinkle in that you need funding. You give examples of the in-kind support you are already receiving. Consistently listing your partners is called social proof. You want your audience to think, "If they are involved, maybe we should be, too."

> *But programs take money... even or especially financial programs.*
>
> *I first want to acknowledge ABC Bank who has been offering our clients tours of their bank and personal assistance in setting up their accounts. For many of our clients, this is the first time they have ever stepped inside a financial institution...*

Many times you need only a short anecdote or a benefit statement with some Story Speak to create a clear, memorable image in your audience's minds. But, sometimes, you need a full-out story. People always ask me "How do you make stories interesting? How is it that with some people you're bored within 30 seconds and others, you hang on their every word no matter how long they speak?" The answer is a skillful use of the Story Elements.

Now, it's time to think about where and how you want to share your stories.

PART SIX
THE SIXTH S:
STORY SHARING

CHAPTER FIFTEEN
CREATING A STORY SYSTEM

When you are ready to share your stories, create a Story System. Think of how you are going to consistently spot, find, gather, refine, and share your stories – first internally and then with a larger audience.

I don't care if you start with summaries of stories on index cards kept in an old shoebox. That, at least, is a start.

I've taught my Story Power for Nonprofits seminars for years. Occasionally, new employees will attend who are from an organization that has attended my workshop in the past. I'm always saddened when *I* wind up telling *them* great stories about their programs instead of the reverse. Without an internal story bank, there was no way for these new employees – who were panicked about presenting at a conference the next week - to know that the organization already had terrific stories that would have worked perfectly for their presentations.

It is important to have an easy way to categorize stories. A number of organizations simply use Excel-type spreadsheets. Each organization has uniquely different categories. A school group, for example, might want to separate G.E.D. stories from E.S.L. stories. Another group needs to distinguish youth stories from adult stories. An arts organization may want to separate concert series stories from outreach stories in the community. Everyone should be able to easily find "Founding" stories, that is, the "Who We Are" and "Why We Do What We Do" stories.

Another suggestion is to write short commentaries on how the stories could be used. For example, "This one is really good for explaining why the November vote is critical," or "This story is good for legislators who like us but need proof of cost savings," or "Press release sent out (date). If a reporter calls, include this story to illustrate why the arts are essential to community safety."

Also, note if you have permission to use a person's name, if written permission is on file, or if the name needs to be changed. Add a field in your spreadsheet that denotes if it's okay to give that person's phone number to a reporter, for example.

There are IT departments or volunteers in some organizations who have created special databases. Others use built-in content management or online connection tools cross-referenced with photographs. Categorizing can get quite elaborate, but it can also be done very simply.

The only unchangeable thing about story gathering is that it won't happen unless someone (or a few people) are put in charge of it and are given some kind of budget for it – a budget of money *and* time. In the end, responsibility and accountability are what get things done.

Don't expect the stories to be there when you need them if you haven't created ways to regularly gather, edit, refine, and bank them.

Collecting stories takes persistence. Ask not once, not twice, but consistently on several different fronts. Solicit stories in your emails or newsletters. Create a "Tell us your story" page on your website. Then, send out postcards that advertise your website's Story Bank and encourage people to submit their stories. At all of your events, announce that you're looking for stories, and read one or have clients present their stories whenever you can.

Learning what makes a good story takes practice. People will rarely tell a fully formed, compelling story right from the start. Most adults start at that 3000-foot level with a distant, nonspecific summary. "Oh, the dance concert was really nice. I enjoyed it." You have to ask questions that will turn those first impressions into concrete, compelling, on-the-ground images.

Remember: you get stories by asking story questions. When gathering stories, the object is to get the people being interviewed to talk in Story Speak – specific sensory details - and to give the highs and lows of an event that can later be crafted into a dynamic Story Structure.

Tell the story of (or include testimonials from) people who submitted stories and had a great experience in the process. This will further encourage people to contribute on your site, in your newsletter, and at your events. "I had such fun remembering the time when…," or "I didn't even realize I knew this until Jake started asking me questions about…"

There is no shortage of material if you will take the time to look and ask for stories. Some organizations actually set aside a couple of times a year and say, "We are going out and getting stories!" They set up interviews. They take along a photographer. They set aside a couple of days, go for broke, and collect, collect, collect.

No one has the time for this. No one! You have reports, and meetings, and networking events so you are going to have to plan for story gathering time. Set the time aside. Treat the time as if you were going to be at an out-of-town conference. You are out of the office. You are story gathering.

And, then, clear time to refine those stories.

Before sharing your stories, take a moment to consider editing. Don't be afraid to play with words. Sometimes, it takes several attempts to figure out exactly what you want to say in a clear and concise way.

When preparing stories, it's important to separate your inner creator from the inner critic. "Play time" in the creation phase is a must. Just because something is already on the page, already in a brochure, or already on the website doesn't mean it's sacred. Maybe it's time to revamp and re-energize tired, worn copy.

The words written about your organization should be inspirational to the people within the organization as well as to the larger community. Writing or telling stories is challenging work. Carol Burnett's quote about giving birth can apply to creative projects of all kinds: "Giving birth is like taking your lower lip and forcing it over your head."

That doesn't mean creating stories isn't also fun and, sometimes, downright awe-inspiring. It just means finding that balance between being satisfied (not over-writing and over-thinking) on one hand and challenging yourself to greater heights on the other.

After the inner creator has had its turn, then (and only then) bring out the inner critic - that part that looks for logical connections, smooth transitions, correct grammar, and just the right word.

Always pay attention to how language affects people. Make a decision today to fall in love with words. It will enrich life beyond measure to notice the art form of language in everyday life. Respect its power. Think of all the governments that won't let newspapers be printed or people speak out. They know words can topple walls and whole regimes.

Even if you are going to use a person's story in his or her own words, you can still rearrange and select what they've said so that the story grabs the audience's attention. Take the transcript of the interview (there are transcript services you can hire via elance.com, guru.com and the like) and edit out the unnecessary parts. Then, rearrange the parts you have left to make the story as interesting as possible. Occasionally, as you look at what's in front of you, you realize you need to fill in additional information. Maybe if there was just one more obstacle, for example, this story would be more gripping. Call the person back and try to fill in any missing details or incidents.

Eventually, show the person what you've created. Most people do not object to a re-arrangement of the timeline of events. For instance, you won't hear, "Oh, no. I talked about the kids' dental clinic *after* I talked about how dental health affects heart health, not before." In the unlikely event that they question the order, simply talk about it and come up with a mutually satisfying structure.

A few notes if you are videotaping stories...

When shooting a video, take the time upfront to pre-interview people whenever possible. In most cases (unless it's a spontaneous, man-on-the-street, interview), it's just not cost effective to figure out if someone has a story while the camera is rolling. The shoot and the subsequent editing will take time and time is money!

Try to arrange one or more conversations with the person being videotaped before the shoot. That way, when the actual interview happens, they are primed and confident. They have already heard several times, "Oh! This is good! This is exactly what I was looking for!"

You want your storytellers to arrive at the shoot positive about their contribution and familiar with the story you're looking for: "Doug, could you tell that story about the break room at your old job? About how the other white men immediately switched from talking politics to talking basketball, thinking that was the way to include you?"

Also, if you are going to include these videos on your site without including your setup questions, then you'll need to explain to those you interview that they need to speak in whole sentences with clearly stated topics because no one will hear the questions they were asked.

In the pre-interview sessions, simply tell the person being interviewed that questions will be cut out and, therefore, he or she will need to include the question in their statement. If to the question, "Did you ever face discrimination on your job as an African American?" Doug simply answered, "Yes, it happened." Trust me, the editing process will be lengthy and painful because no one will know what he's answering "yes" to or what "it" is.

Instead, work with Doug to include your question in his answer, "Sometimes it was subtle but, as the first African American employee, I could see people treating me differently. For instance..."

Try role-playing this "speaking in whole sentences" several times over the phone so that it will minimize the number of times Doug will need to be stopped and started again to give the topic sentence while on the set of the video shoot.

Recently, I stopped by a client's video shoot. My client asked the interviewee, "Was the campaign successful?"

The volunteer answered, "Yes, it was," and proceeded to tell a terrific story. But I knew the plan was to cut out the interviewer's questions and not use any title slides. Therefore, this story might be useless because the audience wouldn't have a clue what the volunteer was talking about.

I later coached my client to instruct the volunteer to speak with a clear starting point that would include my client's question in the answer. Now the video interview could stand-alone. On the next take, the volunteer answered perfectly, "Our volunteer door-to-door campaign was a huge success. Voter registration was up 10%." Now the audience knew what he was talking about and could receive his wonderful story.

People are nervous when the lights and cameras show up. You'll get better stories if the people are familiar with the mechanics of the interview and your confidence in their stories beforehand.

CHAPTER SIXTEEN
ARE YOU NEWSWORTHY?

If I could be a fly on the wall in your office, would I hear you and your co-workers complain that the press doesn't cover your nonprofit's events? Yet, be honest. If a major newspaper or TV station called tomorrow to do a feature story on you, would you have relevant, entertaining, or controversial stories ready to go? Do you have a story about something you're doing *right now* that would tie in with a current news event, that would have an unusual angle and that would be so visual you or they could easily take pictures of it?

There's just no use complaining if, indeed, the media opportunity of a lifetime falls in your lap and you aren't ready to take advantage of it. "C'mon, Sue," you could counter. "How often is that going to happen?"

Well, if you aren't consistently thinking with a media mindset - never. If you don't have a media *plan* or if your organization isn't tuned into what's newsworthy always, every day, all year long, you won't be able to take advantage of *any* opportunities – even the ones that are more likely to come your way.

Pitching a story about hosting an awards banquet or your annual meeting is *not* being ready. Reporters get thousands of invitations and press releases to those kinds of events. They are rarely interesting or unusual enough to be reported in the media.

The media is one of your audiences, just as much as any of your clients, volunteers, potential hires, or donors are. And, as with any audience, you need to enter the conversation that's already going on in their heads. What are they thinking about? What keeps them up at night?

Simply put, media people are anxious about circulation and ratings. In today's constantly changing, competitive landscape, they are worried about staying alive. They're asking, "What are we going to be good at? Where can we make a difference? How are we unique from other media outlets? Where can we win?"

When they read your press release or get a call from you, they only want to know a few things:

One, is your story timely?

Two, is your story interesting? (Which means is it relevant, controversial, or entertaining?)

And, three, is it specific and helpful to *their* audience? In other words, is it their beat? So many reporters tell me something along the lines of: "I am writing about religion and certain nonprofits are sending me education stories. I'm just not going to cover them."

I worked with a nonprofit client to create a year-long media plan for their back-to-work organization. They helped women who had been out of the job market freshen up their computer and other office skills, plus learn how to job hunt and interview.

Because of the shape of the economy at that time, their back-to-work program had received some coverage the year before, but journalists were now looking for a new angle. It was August, and we thought about pitching an Adult Back-to-School story. We did get a little mileage out of that, but the story that really worked was a Back-to-School Clothing story.

The organization decided to sponsor a clothing drive of appropriate work clothes for their clients. Many of the women they worked with couldn't afford business suits and other business attire. Their plea was specific... and visual! Television reporters in particular, but print media, too, need visuals.

The organization pitched a story of a Mom buying her children Back-to-School clothing and, then, stopping by the organization's clothing sale and buying herself a Back-to-Work suit.

Another media outlet traced a designer suit's journey from an expensive boutique to the racks in the organization's basement sale to a woman wearing that business suit as she started her new job. I loved this story – it started global in the high fashion world and its happy ending was truly local!

Help reporters with their jobs. Do some of the thinking, legwork, or the contacting of resources for them. Be a resource to the media, not a bothersome pest who complains about the media not covering you. These are busy people who, with all the cutbacks in personnel, are doing the work that three and four people used to do.

Look at what's going on in your city, in the country, and in the world and ask, "How could we relate to this right now, and how can we suggest an interesting angle?"

Reporters are looking for stories all the time. Check your attitude. Are you defeated before you begin? "They just don't care about work like ours. They never cover us." Or maybe we're back to that sleazy used car salesman image. "I'm not going begging to be covered. I just don't have that kind of hustle." You need an attitude change. Do you believe in what you and your organization do? Then, people deserve to hear about it.

Or maybe your bias is against reporters themselves: "Oh, they're just looking for fluff and glitz." Believe me, there are plenty of reporters looking for real content and meaning. Remember, many of them were inspired to enter journalism for the very same reasons you entered the nonprofit world: they wanted to make a difference.

They believed exposing the truth could have a positive effect. They believed in democracy and the public's right to know. They are, frankly, some of the most idealistic folks I've ever met. You don't need to work with the reporters who, by choice or by need, are working the more superficial beats. You will have plenty of reporters who are interested in your cause - *if* you give them news the way *they* need it.

They can't help you unless you do something that's newsworthy. (Do I need to repeat again that your awards banquet or your annual report is most likely not a hot news item?)

Is there a conflict or some other high emotion or human-interest angle that is a David (your organization) going up against Goliath (a large societal problem)?

Does the issue you're involved with impact the larger community? Is it the first, last, or biggest of something? Is there a twist on an old subject, what we call "man bites dog"?

Does your event have a celebrity involved? (You may find this question dreadful, but you might as well accept what is: celebrities are news in our culture. And there are many wonderful people who have reached celebrity status – those who instantly pique people's interest and curiosity – who care about causes like yours.)

Also, remember that you can be a story *maker*. You can create an event that will give you a story to pitch to the press. If you know, for instance, that a misconception exists that a G.E.D. is something easy to get and you have a good statistic, such as 40% of high school students couldn't even pass the G.E.D., then why not gather a group of high school students to take a G.E.D.-type test and see if you can replicate that 40% statistic?

You could, for example, videotape the high school students' reactions as they come out of the room after taking the test. "Wow, that was harder than I thought!"

Finally, tape their surprise as they get their scores. You could run that video on your website or at a community meeting in addition to presenting the clip to a reporter at graduation time or when the latest statistics on high school reading scores are announced.

CHAPTER SEVENTEEN
DEVELOPING RELATIONSHIPS
WITH MEDIA OUTLETS

Sharing your story is, once again, all about your Story Setup. What do you want to accomplish by pitching this story to the media or by putting it out to the public via your website, newsletter, or social media sites? Are you trying to:

- change an opinion or influence public policy?
- raise the value of your organization?
- drive people to your website?
- And, once there, what is the call to action on each web page? Remember, people don't always enter through your home page. Are you trying to grow your donor base or recruit more volunteers?

Look at your news stories within the context of your organization's ongoing stories. Is the message you're pitching to a reporter consistent with what your organization actually does and how it operates?

Finding the right reporters means truly knowing your base. What does your target audience already read, watch, or listen to? Read the article's byline, or call the TV or radio station to identify who covered a story aimed at your audience. Follow the reporters you want to work with. Keep files of their work. What are they doing now? Notice the length of their pieces and their style. Put their name in Google alerts and track what they write but, also, any stories written about them. Find out what they've done in the past by looking at back issues of the paper.

Remember, if you don't see or hear a byline, you can call the media outlet and ask, "Who did the story on _____?"

Get to know and develop relationships with local reporters. Know the events, charities, and nonprofits that reporters support. Make a plan to meet reporters over shared interests when you aren't asking for anything. Support what *they* care about.

When you feel ready, join PRWire, PRLeads, ProfNet, or HARO (Help a Reporter Out). Offer yourself as an expert on various subjects, and then be ready with short quotes or to direct reporters to other resources. You can become one of their "go-to" people. (If it's not going to be you, carefully choose your spokesperson. Maybe for a particular topic, it would be better to have someone else in your organization do the talking.)

Make a list of events and seasons that relate to your organization or cause. Certain events are repeated – Spring break, health issues, oil and other prices rising, school shootings, outdoor concerts, Ramadan, budget crisis, etc. Be ready ahead of time for when these seasons, anniversary dates, or events occur. Have quotes and resources ready to go.

Create a twelve-month PR calendar. When should your press releases go out (ask or read what reporters prefer in terms of lead time)? Schedule in your follow-up calls. And highlight every article or report in your blog, on your social media sites, and on your website. Tell people that you've been or are going to be covered by the media.

Don't just go for the big national splash. People need to hear about your organization several times over in several formats to break through their information overload. Plus, some of your best supporters are going to come to you because of hearing about you in the local press.

Stay in touch with a reporter by commenting on their stories or sending a note referencing something you know they care about – a sports team, an event at their local school, etc. See if there are ways you can help them with a photo or contact.

If someone called regularly (not as a pest, but every month or so) to help you - really help you - would you not pick up his or her calls? And if, once in a while, the help they were offering had something to do with an event they were involved with, wouldn't you be more than willing to listen to this resource of yours?

Be that resource and, at the same time, minimize any negative associations a reporter might have with you. Pitch on target. Don't waste people's time with something they can't use. If your nonprofit helps battered women, for instance, how long would it take your receptionist to get annoyed if she or he received fifty calls a day asking about environmental issues?

Journalists have memories. When you send an inappropriate pitch to them, it says to them that you don't know what you're doing and that, in fact, you're an amateur. With whom would you rather enter into a relationship: someone who pays attention to your needs or someone who treats you like one of the masses or, even worse, like a piece of furniture to be used only when needed?

Journalists have feelings. They want to feel that they have been considered. Every time you send out a press release, think: who should receive this? Don't try the spaghetti theory of promotion - i.e., throw enough of it against the wall and see what sticks. It's tempting because electronic mail is easy and low in cost. It might make you feel as if you've done something (or a PR service may try to convince you that they've done something) to send out 200 emails. In the end, though, all that really counts is your results. You get results by targeting your story pitches. If you waste a reporter's time, you can get worse than disinterest; you can get a bad reputation.

Also remember that journalists change jobs. You need to update your lists by calling the outlet to double check if reporters are still there and what are their current assignments and contact information. If a media outlet keeps getting messages for reporters who are no longer employed, it lets them know that you are an organization that doesn't do its homework.

Who has the time to do all that updating? Community Media Workshop's Media Directory is a great place to start (http://communitymediaworkshop.org/mediaguide). There are others, such as FinderBinder.com (www.FinderBinder.com). Interns can do regular calling and checking. It all starts with focusing your contact list to begin with, and then keeping an updated selective list after that.

When it's time to contact this targeted media person, learn how to write a succinct, compelling one-page pitch with a headline that grabs and a unique story hook or angle that contains some sensory images that evoke emotion. Check and double-check your facts and contact information.

Remember: you are always selling an interesting angle more than your organization or service. This can sound harsh, but think of it this way: they really don't care about what you do (of course, some do). They care about their readers, viewers, or listeners being interested in your story.

Get out of your business and into theirs. Convince them that your story will keep their audience from turning the page or clicking that remote. Tell them what the segment will look and sound like. "Here are 3 Lively Show Ideas." Don't forget - you can be a story maker by offering a giveaway, running a contest, or doing some sort of demonstration on their show.

Put your pitch in the body of the email. Don't make reporters open an attachment (picture them at their computers with 600 emails to open). You can include the attachment on nicer paper and fonts for them later, if they're interested. But let them get to your enticing story idea quickly.

Use their name in the subject line, and give them a quick way to know what your pitch is about *and how it relates to them*. "Bill, timely story: rise in homelessness" or "Joan, local story, Chamber of Commerce hosts Habitat for Humanity volunteers"

If you use a news wire such as Media Distribution Services (MDS) or PR Newswire, make sure they understand your media focus. Don't just walk away after hiring them thinking everything is covered. You still need to maintain a watchful eye that your pitches are going to the right outlets and to the right people. Don't get impressed by numbers. Anyone can send out tons of emails. Look for results.

Here's an organized sequence I like to use when contacting reporters: email first. Then, leave a voicemail once. After that, call several times without leaving a voicemail. If you don't make contact after several tries, start the cycle again and send an email.

Be persistent and follow up. If you do make contact, don't say, "Did you get the material we sent?" Instead, reference that you sent them information previously. "I'm following up with you now because (timely incident is happening)."

Have a reason each time you call them. Pitch your idea as helpful to them. Talk or write less about you and more about their audience. "One reason your audience might be interested in this topic now is…"

This should be a no-brainer, but journalists tell me it happens all the time: Don't call print journalists at the end of their day when they're on deadline. And don't call during the time a radio or TV show airs. Actually, don't call for an hour and a half before a show or an hour after. The times for live programs are usually listed on a station's website or you can get the times from the receptionist.

When you call, don't start with a weak, "Sorry to bother you" or "Sorry to take your time." It is the reporters' job to listen to story ideas. When leaving a voicemail or talking on the phone, stand up and smile into the phone. We lose a lot of the vibrancy of our voices over the phone, so you have to add the sizzle back in.

Turn off call waiting and use a landline whenever possible, not a cell phone (unless you can count on exceptional reception). Pick a time and place when you can eliminate the distraction of crying babies, barking dogs, and zooming traffic.

Remember, you're talking to a media person, so keep this in your mind - I'm here to help him/her. Do they need what I have? You're trying to see if there's a match. That's all. You are not asking for anything. You're not begging. You are simply saying, "I think I have something that will help you reach your readers/listeners/viewers. Does it?" (If not, no big deal.)

When you call, have a four sentence, *scripted* pitch ready to go. "I enjoyed your piece on _____ (one sentence – sincerely build rapport). I'm a (title/description). I propose you do a story about _____ or I have an idea for a similar type of story with a different angle _____. Your readers/listeners will laugh/learn/wonder/question when they hear/read about _____. Is this the kind of story that would appeal to your audience? Shall I send you more information? Would you like to schedule an interview?"

If they reject you, don't take it personally. *Learn* why this story wasn't a good fit. Don't slink away. Ask them: "No problem. Just so I can be more on target next time, why do you feel that this story doesn't work for your show/magazine/column?"

If they can't do a story just about you, suggest a roundup story. "I can give you the name of several other organizations that do similar work. Would that be of interest to your readers to find out about several resources in our area?" Suggest photos. Be ready to send them. Before every storytelling festival, we did a photo shoot of the tellers in various poses with onions (we were The Wild Onion Storytelling Festival): sporting flamenco dance poses with green onions in our teeth like roses, large onions being stared at as if they were crystal balls, etc. Those photos always appeared in the papers and on TV.

When you're finally interviewed or you appear on a radio or TV show, don't turn the show into a commercial for your organization or cause. That's the host's job. Talk about *their* audience. "People often wonder how to solve _____. Well, what we have found that works for most people in the caller's predicament is _____."

Have a clear idea of how you'd like to be described. Be ready with short facts, quotes, and "sound bites" written or spoken as they would be for this reporter's audience in his or her style and length.

Many times, my press releases have been published verbatim because I wrote it in the reporter's style. These are busy people! Whenever you can, do their work for them and get the extra bonus of having a measure of control on how you are presented. Don't sit back and *hope* they get you right.

Again, when you're interviewed, learn to speak in quotable sound bites and avoid superlative statements. Finally, this goes without saying, but if your photo will be taken or you're going to be on TV or video, wear the right clothing, suitable for their audience and your story pitch.

CHAPTER EIGHTEEN
FOLLOWING-UP AND LEVERAGING
YOUR MEDIA EXPOSURE

After your story is printed or aired, send a thank you note and a small, memorable gift. Find out a reporter's or host's favorites: brownies? A certain musician's CD? A book by their favorite author?

After you're interviewed, ask them: "Just so I know, is there any way we could work together even better in the future? Is there any way I could have been more helpful to you leading up to this interview or during the interview?"

Their job is not to promote you, but it's okay to ask them, "Do you know of other hosts/reporters who would benefit from this type of presentation/information for their audience?" "Would you suggest I let the national network know about the unique angle we took on this topic?" If they say, "Yes" it's quite appropriate to call the national producer and say, "So and so radio host at XYZ station suggested I call you. We just did a show on...."

While you're there (and assuming the interview went well), you can softly pitch: "When you said _____, (or when that call-in guest asked...) it got me thinking. Would you be open to a few ideas of how we could extend this topic in a new way for your audience in the future?"

If you are developing an on-going relationship with this person (and you are, right?), after you've been of service to them several times you can suggest being a repeat guest for a weekly/monthly segment or guest blog.

Leverage your PR. Frame your articles. Send your write-ups to potential donors and volunteers, *and* to the reporter/host/producer you just worked with. Take a photo of yourself with them and put it in nice frame. I've been surprised to come back six months or even a year later to a radio or TV stations and see my photo up on their wall. Just as your audience needs repeat impressions to remember you, reporters need ongoing contact to bring you to mind. There's nothing like having your sweet mug smiling on them day after day, the two of you looking like best buddies.

Put everything on your website. Have a clear, useable media section – reporters like to see what other reporters have written about you. Use media quotes in your collateral materials – for instance, in your brochures and on the back of your business cards. Then, ask for testimonials from people who have read or heard about you. Use these testimonials for yourself – on your websites, brochures, business cards, etc. – but also send the testimonials to your media contact. "Look at the kind of comments we received from our patrons after they saw me on your show. Looks like we hit the mark!"

Write what you've learned about this reporter, producer, or host in the contact database that you already have (You're keeping a media database, right?). Add any likes and dislikes that you learned about them, especially anything you learned about how they like to work, how they like to receive press releases, times they don't like to be called, etc. (These are questions you can ask after an interview when you're inquiring how you might have served them better.) Put each media person into your contact calendar and make a plan to stay in touch.

Don't get seduced into thinking that one big media splash will set up your organization for life. First of all, even if you do get large national exposure, *you* have to be ready to extend the benefits from the publicity. In a day or so, the media will have moved on. Second, it is the steady, repeated impressions that cause people to remember your organization. Be ready to jump on a big opportunity. When it comes to the media, the old axiom "slow and steady wins the race" should be your guiding image.

CHAPTER NINETEEN
A SOCIAL STRATEGY

Obviously, when you think about the 6th S – Story Sharing – considering your Social Media strategy is a must. I'm not going to go into detail on the various platforms you might use. For one thing, if I did, this book would need to be updated every few months. (Anyone remember Friendster?)

I'd rather discuss how to *think* about social media. There are plenty of resources that will help you to design your customized social media plan. (But you do understand that you need a plan, right? Not a try-a-little-of-this-and-that strategy. If you use the shotgun approach, you will easily decide that "social media doesn't work" and be left behind.)

Social Media is a done deal and it has forever changed how all of us do or need to do marketing. Again, if I quoted exact numbers, I would be outdated before I even finish writing this sentence. Let's just know we're talking about billions of internet users! Do you understand how many people "billions" is? Truly, we can barely wrap our minds around it.

Before internet marketing, letting folks know of the existence of your organization and what it does was a one-way street - a glorified brochure where people could read about you and get your contact information. We had the smallest hint of what the internet was going to become as we found ourselves using our yellow pages less and less.

Then, I remember looking up restaurant menus before I went out to eat. Later, going to my computer for movie times instead of looking in the newspaper. Still, just inklings of how powerful the internet was going to become.

Now, of course, the uses for the internet and the degree of connectivity has exploded. That's the good news. The bad news is that you might be feeling a little overwhelmed. Of course you are. So let's just cover a couple of basics:

- One, you already know how to use social media because social media simply mimics how people socialize in everyday life. Unless you're living under a rock (I just don't meet too many anti-social people in the nonprofit world), you know how to be social. You know how to meet other people, how to help them get to know you, and how to trade information, resources, and invitations.

- Two, the interactive web technology of today and the applications of the future have made it possible for you to do what you already do times a thousand.

That's it. That's all that's going on.

The same attributes of social discourse exist on the internet as in live, person-to-person socializing:

- We are social animals.
- We want people to know us, like us, and trust us so they feel good about being with us.
- Branding, once more, is simply other people recognizing your organization and feeling good about you when they do.
- The good feelings - the knowing, the liking, and the trusting build over time.
- It's useful to be known over the internet because as people get to know, like, and trust you they will come to your events, volunteer, donate, defend you, support legislation that helps you, and tell others about you.

There are only three locations you need to think about when designing a plan to socialize with people on the internet:

- One, invite people to your home (your website) and your events.
- Two, meet people where they already are. You know your audience of donors, volunteers, clients, and community people. You've done your research. You know where they mingle. Rather than wandering the streets of the internet, go for the sure thing - the place where you know they are.
- Three, listen in on the sites where they talk about their experiences with nonprofits. Listen in on what they are saying about you and, if needed, respond appropriately.

One – Invite People to Your Home

When you invite people to your physical house, you have a purpose in mind. You are going to watch a sporting event, or you are going to play cards, and so on. You need to know the purpose of your website – why you are inviting people there – and, then, deliver. When people come to your physical house to watch the Superbowl, you best turn on the game. If the monthly bridge club shows up, you better pull out the cards.

So what is your purpose? Why do you want to have a website? Because everybody does isn't a good enough reason.

The great thing about inviting people to your home website is that:

a. Search engines that can help people find your organization. Plus, you give out your home address (via your web URL) on your newsletter, business cards, and so on.

b. With today's technology, your home site can stay current and change just as you do as a person – that keeps you interesting, that makes people want to associate with you. It used to be that you'd have to pay a webmaster $100 every time you wanted something changed on your website, but now you can make those changes yourself. Just as you try to have something new at every physical open house, you keep your home website lively and new. You give people a reason to come back to it. You are always inviting people to a live event, a teleseminar or webinar, announcing a new blog post, article, or report and so on.

c. You have more control in your own home. Your guests can stay all night. You have plenty of time to say what you want to say. You aren't limited by 140 characters or other length restrictions. You have plenty of room, so you can even pull out all your old photographs or show your teapot collection. If they are in your home, they can ask questions and learn things about you they didn't know before. You can invite them to other events you're part of, share knowledge and resources, and tell them about other people they should know. Before the internet, when your communication was one-way with your audience, you could print only so many posters, postcards, or annual reports. Now, your "poster" or "postcard" invitation can be seen on your website and shared with thousands. You can invite your audience to download your reports with no printing costs to you. You don't only give them a resource name and contact information, you give them a link. It's as if you take your friends by the hand and walk them right to another organization that can help them. People see your organization as one of the helpful ones.

d. Plus, now you can track if your audience received and read your invitation or went to that other resource. Everything can be measured on the internet. For example, suppose you are an arts organization, and you had a live, physical open house. At this open house, there were different displays in different rooms. As you stood and greeted people, you might get a sense that the photography display was a huge hit, but the crafts room was hardly used. Someone else in your organization might say, "No. When I walked in the crafts room there were at least five families in there. We *have* to have a crafts room at our next event." Short of having people with counters stationed in each room, you couldn't be sure. However, on the internet, you can measure how many folks come into each room on your site, where they come from, how long they stay, and what actions they take while there.

e. New technology makes it possible to have conversations. You can hear what people are saying about you and talk directly to them as well.

f. By offering your audience something they want in exchange for their email, you can build a verifiable, opt-in list which gives you permission to stay in touch with them.

Because you know how to be social in real life, you know what *not* to do when socializing on the internet:

- *Don't* talk only about yourself. Watch that you aren't falling into boring, self-aggrandizing chatter. Show interest in others. Ask people about themselves and listen. Be aware of how your conversations are being received. Search for topics that would be interesting to the people with whom you are talking. At the other extreme, if you invited people to your home and you said nothing, how anxious would people be to come to another one of your parties? You'll hear the phrase "on the internet, content is king/queen". You must be interesting. Don't let that frighten you. "Interesting" is whatever your audience cares about.

- *Don't* lose contact. If you have made great connections with new contacts, take care to get their business cards so that you can stay in touch. Then, make a plan to build relationships. Of course, you don't take peoples' business cards and start calling them five times a day. Get to know them and help them to get to know you with bite-size, consistent contacts. For example, give free tip sheets, and get their email addresses. Send them a special report. Next, invite them to a free teleseminar that goes into more depth on a topic you know they care about. From time to time, throw in an invitation that is simply entertaining. Let them know you're a fun person to be around. Ask them for their opinion on the subjects you're discussing and any other ways you could be of help to them. With each request for participation, offer them something for their time. Your contact with them should be about one thing: How can I serve you? Plan to let the trust and participation evolve.

- *Don't* try to stay in contact with everyone or you will drive yourself crazy. If there isn't a connection with someone, don't waste your time and energy. When people come to your house, they may invite you to their home or tell you about something in which they are involved. You can't accept every invitation that you receive. You are always foremost strategic about how you use your most precious commodity, your time, so that it is mutually beneficial to everyone. Pick one to three top social medial sites to be involved in (because that's where your audience is), and get to know those sites really, really well. Constantly measure your results. See which sites and other links get the most traffic, and concentrate your energies there before adding anything new.

- You *don't* invite people over to your house under the guise of socializing and then start selling them real estate, cleaning products, or plastic food storage systems. People don't want to be sold. But if you are interesting, if you've shared information or referrals about something they're interested in, then they might just be interested, eventually, if you have a relationship with them. Build relationships and, at the right point, tell them more about what *you* have - your programs, your donor levels, etc. Always be upfront when you are asking something of another person.

Two – Go to Where People Already Are

You wouldn't meet many people if you just waited for everyone to show up at your house. Some people will just never get off the couch and come your way, but they may saunter over to the corner coffee shop every Saturday afternoon.

On the internet, you must go to where your audience spends time. We're always coming back to our Story Setup. Have you done your research on your audience in terms of their web behavior? Where do they already interact? When they are looking for an organization like yours, what key phrases are they putting into Google? (You'd better have those keywords all over your site, or they'll just never find you.)

I caution you again to be strategic. In real life, you can't accept every dinner invitation or go to every professional conference, can you? If you want to talk to other folks interested in early childhood education, you don't go to the plumbers' conference. You *do* go to the annual Headstart meeting.

Choose one or two social media sites and get really good at seeing how they work and how best to network on them. Many of us go to the same conferences year after year. We know which events at the conference are best for networking. Make your choices on the web the same way. Go back to your Story Setup. Whom do you want to reach and why? Then ask, "*Where* are they?"

Remember everything is measurable on the web. You can see which of your efforts are driving the most traffic back to your site and, once there, if people are "converting" - taking action on your site and becoming more involved with your organization. If you regularly gather these statistics and learn how to interpret them, you'll be able to determine if your energies are best spent guest blogging or refreshing your Pinterest boards.

In real life, when you go to the places where your audience already interacts – conferences, meetings, classes, social events – you observe a certain kind of social etiquette. It's the same in the virtual world. For example, you don't just talk about yourself. You give useful information. You offer ways for people to get in touch with you if they want to know more. For example, when you make comments on other people's blogs or social media posts, be helpful and include your website. Don't, however, simply promote yourself and your cause.

Think of it this way: when you go to physical conferences and the like, you meet a lot of people. Often, you leave with a stack of business cards and maybe even a list of attendees. How many times do we follow up on those contacts or even enter them into our database? It's not so easy to do, right?

But on many social media sites all that data entry is done for us. Once people follow us or we follow them, we're connected.

Maybe you had even planned to extend your reach at a conference. For example, you paid to have a flier about your cause in each attendee's welcome bag. But you can't know for sure if people even looked at the flier. Again, the wonderful thing about the internet is that you can measure who opened your flier or invitation. Plus, those people can instantly talk back to you. And, depending upon the platform, some social media sites allow all of their friends and contacts to listen in as they talk to you. Without you doing anything, their friends and contacts instantly hear about you as well.

The internet is like physical networking on steroids. You have your friends, but (depending on the platform) you also have instant access to your friends' friends.

Each time you meet people on social media sites, article directories, and the like, you invite them back to your house. Driving people back to your site is one of your primary objectives in marketing on the web. You drive people back to your home base because you can share so much more there about your organization. You always have something exciting going on – something you're offering, something you're inviting people to online and in real life. You have something to give so that you can capture their contact information and build your database. As a friend of mine says, you are developing your herd and putting a fence around that herd. If you truly serve your herd, that database is your most valuable asset. You can create a *community* that is devoted to you because you are devoted to them. You get a reputation as an organization people can rely on, a group they want to keep in touch with and follow.

Three – Listen to What Others Are Saying

Sometimes, we get a little insecure around people, yes? We meet people, see a strange look on their face, and we wonder if we said something wrong. Did we offend them in some way, or are they just having a bad day?

Another great thing about social media – you can listen in and see what people are saying about you as well what they're saying about themselves. You read their short message, and they mention they have five huge deadlines this week. That's probably why they haven't gotten back to you. If someone writes a negative review about your organization, you can respond and clear up any misunderstanding immediately. I know that none of us likes to hear anything negative, but people may have been saying these things for a very long time and you never heard their opinions before. It's better to know. When the person who wrote the negative review is satisfied with how you've handled their complaint, ask him or her to write about their positive experience on the same review site. Voila! Instant credibility!

One clear rule of internet social etiquette: *Don't* attack. If you hear that someone is mistaken about you, correct them right away without blame or judgment. If you've made a mistake, admit it and tell people what you are doing to correct it. Then make plans to do better in the future. Take the time to rebuild trust and monitor if that trust is indeed rebuilding. Always be the bigger person because counter-attacking will never be productive.

At certain times, know when the wisest thing is not to say anything at all. It's a fine balancing act. Again, have an "emergency" media plan in place and someone responsible for it. Play out the "What if?" scenarios so that you know how to respond. The new technology is instant communication. If you have to wait to run every internet interaction by your Executive Director, you'll be too late. Preparation for "crisis communication" or disgruntled customers is essential. Be proactive, not reactive.

Today, you can literally reach the world for relatively little money in two-way conversations where you can also listen in on your audiences' conversations about themselves and about you. Have clear outcomes in mind and a plan to engage happily within this ever-expanding virtual community.

FINALLY...

The *6 S Story Power System*™ is there for you for only one purpose – so that the people you want to reach can know your organization, recognize it, and feel good about you.

Because your entire intent has been to live your mission and to serve your clients, your staff, your volunteers, your donors and your community (including the media, the legislators, other nonprofits and so on), you must learn to tell your stories in such compelling ways that people will come to know, like, and trust you. Powerful, captivating storytelling is often how people become involved with you and stay involved.

Businesses, of course, need their customers' involvement to stay profitable. Nonprofits are quickly realizing that they need a solid, dedicated, and forceful base as well. Their good works and good intentions are not enough to capture people's attention and commitment.

Nonprofits must slice through the information clutter to be seen and heard. A story well told is one of the most effective tools of communication that nonprofits have. It has been my honor, over the last thirty years, to work with some of the most outstanding nonprofits in the U.S. and abroad. My wish for you is that you begin to recognize all the incredible stories that already exist within your organization and that this book, *Compelling Stories, Compelling Causes,* is the start of a dedicated practice to improving and sharing your inborn storytelling skill.

ABOUT THE AUTHOR

Susan O'Halloran has been *the* story consultant to Fortune 500 as well as nonprofit organizations for the last 30 years. Her *6S Story Power System* has been used by hundreds of organizations to raise their profile in the community, to attract quality volunteers, to capture the attention of the press, and to show donors how their contributions make a positive and significant difference. For her storytelling in the film medium, Sue is the recipient of national and international video/film honors - including awards of excellence in training from the CINDY competition, the U.S. Industrial Film Festival, and the Los Angeles Film Advisory Board. In addition, Sue produces story theater pieces such as *White, Black and Brown: Tribes & Bridges At the Steppenwolf Theatre* and *More Alike Than Not: Stories of Three Americans – Catholic, Jewish and Muslim.*

Sue has been seen on such media programs as *PBS, ABC Nightline,* and has been interviewed by *The New York Times* and the *Chicago Tribune.* About her storytelling skills, *The Chicago Reader's Critic Choice* said, "O'Halloran has mastered the Irish art of telling stories that are funny and heart-wrenching at the same time."

Within her own storytelling profession, the National Storytelling Network, she has received the Leadership and Service and the Circle of Excellence Oracle Awards. One organization's newsletter stated: "Sue's presentation was a brilliant synthesis of information. She made us feel that together we could do anything!"

O'Halloran Diversity Productions helps organizations reduce turnover and attrition, avoid PR nightmares and remove unconscious, unintended barriers to productivity. Susan lives in Evanston, IL and can be found at: www.SusanOHalloran.com.

RESOURCES

Susan has delivered seminars for Nonprofits through the Community Media Workshop for over a decade and highly recommends all their courses for nonprofits:

www.newstips.org and www.communitymediaworkshop.org

For a free poster of the *6 S Story Power System* go to:
www.SusanOHalloran.com/6s

Made in the USA
Columbia, SC
22 January 2020